A
LITTLE
JOURNEY

A LITTLE JOURNEY

JUNE STRONG

REVIEW AND HERALD PUBLISHING ASSOCIATION
Washington, DC 20039-0555
Hagerstown, MD 21740

This book was
Edited by Gerald Wheeler
Designed by Richard Steadham
Cover art by Lou Skidmore
Type set: 11/12 Century School Book

PRINTED IN U.S.A.

Library of Congress Cataloging in Publication Data
Strong, June.
A little journey.

1. Strong, June. 2. Seventh-day Adventists—United States—Biography. I. Title.
BX6193.S77A35   1985   286.7'32'0924 [B]   8413361

ISBN 0-8280-0236-3

*I dedicate this book
to my daughter
LORI
who stayed behind
and did all the domestic things
so I could go.*

PREFACE

This book is the account of a search. I have chosen to share it because I believe that many men and women come to the same place in which I found myself in my late forties. Too old to continue to ignore the persistent issues of our existence, we deal with them in different ways. I chose to isolate myself. To go far, but not too far. No, I was not running away. Searching for something lost, I found instead something that had been with me all along.

Sometimes a part of me wants to go back. Back to the misty mornings when spruces loomed black against the fog, and the road curved out of sight into mysterious places.

As I seek to put it all down, I invite you to come with me. There were times when I was very lonely and would have welcomed your presence.

The author

THE FIRST DAY

1 The idea began to germinate in my mind during the summer. Our house was full of family and activity, my schedule hectic, and now and then when I felt I was splintering in all directions, I would retreat into a fantasy of hiking up the Maine coast alone for a few days. Over the years I had found such daydreams more beneficial than tranquilizers. Only this time, when September arrived and we all settled into our fall routines, the dream didn't die. My life resembled a snarled and knotted ball of yarn. It needed attention. I longed to find a place that offered time and quiet for the painstaking task of unraveling, for picking at the knots.

Now, here in the sunlight, high above the clouds between Buffalo and Boston, I am astonished at what I am doing. Only moments ago I left my husband and youngest daughter in a downpour at the Buffalo airport.

I have embarked upon a journey. A little journey in terms of miles, but hopefully a longer journey into the complex corridors of my life. Now 49 years old, I want to back off from all that is familiar and gain perspective. I have lived through a turbulent reevaluation of woman's role. It has only nicked my small world, but no woman has passed through it unscathed. Although I have raised six children, four of them adopted, I know less about child raising than when I began twenty years ago. The only thing I am sure of now is that it is difficult. That with the best of intentions one can make horrendous mistakes. That watching one's child struggle to find his identity apart from his parents is infinitely more painful than bringing him into life. Yet for all that, the raising of a child is life's ultimate experience.

Four days ago Don and I celebrated our thirtieth anniversary, and I want to think about our marriage a bit in the next few days. I felt dreadful when I left him behind at the airport this morning. That is one of the reasons I am going—I have grown so dependent upon his care. I must find out if I can still function on my own.

In the past ten years I have authored a few reasonably successful Christian books and done a monthly column for a national magazine. It still astonishes me that out of my mundane housewifely existence, this green shoot of creativity sprang up. I count it as a little surprise package from God.

And speaking of God, I have also set out upon this journey to refresh my relationship with Him. We too have been together nearly thirty years. Or, I guess, He's *always* been with me, but I only became aware of my need for Him in my life when I was 19. Even that relationship has become battered and frayed, though I expect His end of it is in good repair.

I shall be flying on from Boston to Portland, Maine. There, I will board a bus for Rockland, where I shall start walking up the coast along Penobscot Bay, trudging from town to town with the traffic of U.S. Route 1 whizzing along between me and sea. I am both scared and eager.

For a time I hesitated to ask Don if I might go. He does not like me away for a day, to say nothing of a week. I feared he would interpret my need to get away as a reflection on our marriage. As I know full well, he has no such needs himself. Don goes at life with a reasonable simplicity, never letting it nibble at his composure. He would not dream of taking a journey unnecessarily without me.

So I began to toss out little jokes about going to Maine and hiking along the shore. At first our sons and daughters laughed. Young men and women, they were long used to Mom's flighty plans that seldom materialized. But Don didn't laugh. He just kept quiet. It's a very successful tactic. Usually I burn out in the talking stage. But this time I didn't. And after a while the children stopped laughing and Don began to ask me why.

Unfortunately I couldn't give him a good answer. Not the neat, logical explanation he would have liked, anyhow. But I did the best I could, and he listened and tried to understand, because that's the kind of marriage we have and the kind of person he is.

And when our anniversary came along, he gave me the plane tickets, the credit card, and the traveler's checks for the trip. Also he kept his cool when all our friends chided, "Why are you letting her do this harebrained thing?"

It is now 9:00 P.M. The first day of my journey is nearly over. Somehow I made it in and out of Boston airport alone. Always in such situations I've trotted cheerfully and blindly along behind Don. Consequently, I have become filled with traveling fears. Fears that I can't find my way around in airports or will miss my plane. I have actually refused speaking engagements because I disliked flying and I panic in airports. But it went OK today at Logan, even though I had to go out of the Allegheny sector and take a shuttle bus to another part of the airport. My time was limited. Just the kind of setup that keeps me home on the farm. But I asked questions, moved fast, and all went well. (Exactly how Don has always told me I would function if cast upon my own resources, but I dared not believe him.) When I settled into my seat on the Portland-bound Delta I felt good.

A little old lady rode the shuttle bus with me. She had a cane and a bag and should never have been in a big city alone. Though no longer agile, she was rich in spirit and spunk. Since she was looking for the Delta boarding area too, I took her bag and towed her along as best I could, but her days of hurrying had long passed. Though my time was running out, I determined to stick with her. I didn't have the heart to tell her her plane was already boarding.

"I'm heading for Bangor," she said breathlessly. "My husband was a professor at the university there for many years, and I'm going back to visit friends."

"I'm going to hike up the coast of Maine for a few days," I said, as though it were a perfectly normal thing for a middle-aged housewife to do.

She stopped dead still and looked at me, her wrinkled face crinkling with delight. "You lucky girl," she beamed. "May the sun shine on you every day." I'd liked to have taken her with me as a reminder that youth is a state of mind. Besides, not many people called me girl anymore. Finally I found an attendant with a wheelchair, and the last I saw of her she was spinning merrily along the corridor, turning to wave her thanks.

Upon arriving in Portland, I checked in at the Holiday Inn on Spring Street, where I had reservations, and set out to explore the town. It is a small city in which you can get around on your two feet. An old, old city. Many houses in the harbor area are three stories high, have peeling paint, and are obviously vacant on the upper floors. They must be frightfully expensive to heat and maintain. Yet it's these very buildings that lend atmosphere to the city, and certainly some must rate among the most beautiful in America, preserving the earliest type of architecture in the country. To my delight, I discovered that two of the finest were designed by John Kimball, Jr. It thrilled me to find my family name connected with such impressive structures.

Walking down Congress Street on a warm September afternoon with the gulls wheeling overhead and the tang of sea air in one's nostrils is a most pleasant experience. The wide sidewalks have been restored to their original brick construction, and large cement planters overflow with flowers. There is little activity upon the streets this Sunday afternoon. A few scruffy characters huddle in a doorway, smelling bad and eyeing each passerby. I follow a middle-aged couple down the street. They are in a romantic mood, and she clings unsteadily to his arm. Her voice is shrill and her makeup too heavy. They are both pathetic and funny.

The upper classes of Portland are, obviously, home enjoying the bright fall weekend, leaving the streets to the drunks and me. Nevertheless, I am enjoying every moment. I could easily while away the entire afternoon sitting on a bench in Monument Square, but then I would miss the art museum. And that would be unfortunate, for Portland's Museum of Art, though small, is a most interesting place. Among the canvases by Stuart, Homer, Wyeth, and Sargent are portraits of those progressive men who made Portland a thriving town through their enterprising pursuits upon the high seas. They were portly and proud, those men who amassed some of the first fortunes in America. The artists caught that confidence and preserved it for me to enjoy more than 150 years later. The museum has paintings of their wives and children, too. And exhibits of the delicate Oriental bowls and urns with which the captains gifted their wives upon return from afar. I am nearly staggering under nostalgia for that golden age when I happen upon some typewritten copy posted near the exit. The sheets reproduce part of a letter written by the Reverend Edward Payson to his parents on December 28, 1807.

It seems President Thomas Jefferson had initiated measures culminating in the embargo act of December 22, 1807, which forbade all foreign trade by American vessels. The letter read:

"A large number of the most wealthy merchants have already failed and numbers more are daily following so that we are threatened by universal bankruptcy. All confidence is lost. No man will trust his neighbor, but everyone takes even his brother by the throat saying, 'Pay me that thou owest.'"

Later, William Willis observed of the period that "poor Portland and all its noble merchant princes were cast into the dust. The wharves became silent and solitary, grass grew in our streets, mechanic shops were closed, and the town, desolated by an utter prostration, was clothed in sackcloth.

"The palaces had to be abandoned by their luxurious occupants, and many of those who had fared sumptuously every day were glad to partake of the humble bowls of soup which were freely furnished at the public expense."

So much for the glory of man!

Now I think of all this as I sit in my room on the seventh floor at the Holiday Inn watching dusk fall over the harbor. In my imagination I try to see a great sailing ship coming into port with its cargo of exotic wares. I think about the women who rustled along the brick sidewalks in their Oriental silks, and how humbling it must have been to have stood in line for that charity soup.

It feels good just to sit and look out the window,

letting my thoughts wander as they will. I realize how seldom I do this. My time is scheduled down to the last moment, the pace frantic. Even on this journey I have set a goal for each day. Camden by nightfall, Lincolnville Beach by nightfall . . .

Somehow I seem incapable of relaxing. Even as I sit before the window viewing the harbor, I'm feeling guilty because I had planned to write a long-overdue letter.

Maybe when I go home, I'll take a half hour every day in which to be frivolous. But there I go, charting and making a timetable. You can't schedule leisure. Perhaps one must be born to it—and I was not. Anyhow, I think right now I'll defy the genes and take a long hot bath instead of writing the letter.

Lights come on all over the harbor. It is very beautiful. I am lonely. That is an interesting discovery, for I had looked forward most of all to the solitude this journey would provide.

THE SECOND DAY

2 I rise at 8:00 A.M., almost loath to leave the security of this comfortable room overlooking Portland's foggy harbor. The airport, my umbilical cord to home, is only a taxi fare away.

Today I shall taste the adventure for which I have come. I have no idea where I shall sleep tonight. Or eat. Or whether or not I can hike full pack without succumbing to blisters and fatigue.

Whatever made me think it was necessary to find out?

But the bus for Rockland does not leave till 1:00 P.M., so I still have the morning. Time to back out.

I read my Bible. Pray. The habits of a lifetime. Then off to breakfast and more sightseeing. In a small restaurant I order scrambled eggs, muffins, and hot chocolate. Somehow, I'm not hungry and only nibble at it. Uneasy, I cannot imagine why. Perhaps I shall always be uneasy away from Don. Maybe that's what happens in a good marriage. The Bible says that "a man shall leave his father and his mother, and shall cleave unto his wife: and they shall be one flesh" (Gen. 2:24). I think I am afraid of that. It's like melting into someone else, until in the mingling one's original self is lost. But at any rate, I'm presently experiencing a strange new sensation, as though living, pulsing threads of my being are tearing away from some vital source.

I wander down Congress Street not really expecting the Wadsworth-Longfellow house to be open, for it's off-season. But it is, and the tour is just beginning. My depression lifts immediately, and I am caught up in the guide's commentary as we move from room to room. The past is fascinating. It doesn't have to be Longfellow's. My neighbor's great-grandmother's will do just as well. But here I am looking at a small portable desk that Longfellow used for writing when he traveled—an elegant piece of woodwork that historians believe the poet purchased from a sailor who had produced the masterpiece to pass the time at sea. The writer in me responds. I'd count it a good piece of luck to own such an item myself.

Totally absorbed, I admire the wallpaper designs, while keeping one ear tuned to the guide's comments. Over the law office fireplace hangs a picture of Annie Longfellow, sister of Henry. She was born in the house and lived there more than eighty years, leaving only for a brief period during her three-year marriage. Her young husband died of typhoid. Another picture of her hangs in the hall, this one in old age. It was she who gave the house as a memorial, an innovation in her day. She was lovely in her youth. I wondered why she never remarried. Had the years been long and lonely, or had she sensibly filled them with work and small pleasures?

The wall in an upstairs bedroom displayed bills from Henry's years at Bowdoin College. Also those of his older brother Stephen. Tuition was $8 per month, and Stephen often ran up nearly half again that amount in fines for skipping prayers and recitations, for neglecting to turn in papers, et cetera. Later, the guide said, Stephen drank himself to death. Isn't it strange, I thought—two boys with the same background, training, and heritage. One totally undisciplined. The other highly creative with his life under control. Down in the law office as we were leaving, the guide commented briefly that Stephen, as number one son, had been compelled to study law in the family tradition, while Henry, as second son, had been free to choose his lifework. Maybe that explained a few things.

Henry had two wives. The first, a pretty woman, died from a miscarriage on a trip to Europe. The second burned to death when her long skirt caught fire upon the hearth. In his attempts to save her, Henry acquired bad burns about the face and hands. To cover the scars, he grew the beard that he wore throughout the remainder of his life.

The Longfellow family certainly knew all about tragedy. I felt their sorrows yet in the tidy, sparse rooms.

Before leaving the house I sought, and gained, permission to walk alone in the small walled garden behind it. It's a quiet spot of peace and sunlight, surrounded by the commerce of a busy city. Narrow brick paths wander beneath the trees, and one would not be surprised to come upon the poet seated on a bench, creating a rhyme.

After buying a tiny sterling spoon to add to Amy's collection, I hurried back to the Holiday Inn to gather my things and head for the bus station, which, fortunately, was less than a block away. I had not been on a bus in years, yet found in the waiting room the same dingy atmosphere I recalled from the bus stations of my boarding school days. Gum wrappers, cigarette butts, and dirt. The Greyhound pulled out of Portland at 1:00 P.M. Refusing to fret for the two-hour journey, I took my Bible from my pack. I had come on this trip determined to unpeel the accumulated layers of conventional religion and see if there was anything underneath. People consider me a "religious person"— whatever that is. They treat me like a religious person—are careful not to swear in my presence, and do not tell me off-color stories. But all of this, of course, does not make me a religious person. Something alive and vital has to be going on between a human and his God to be authentic. Lately I've felt like a fake. A reproduction of a Christian. This is not because of any lack on God's part. His contribution to the partnership remains constant. I know He has not divorced me anymore than Don would divorce me from our marriage if I developed a spell of poor cooking or complained that I didn't "feel" like a good wife anymore. It is *I* who have reached a plateau and cannot seem to get off. I have a few old sins I have carried for so many years that I almost despair of ever leaving them behind.

Bouncing in the cramped seat of the bus, I puzzle over John 8:32 and 36: "And ye shall know the truth, and the truth shall make you free." "If the Son, therefore, shall make you free, ye shall be free indeed."

That is what I wanted—to be free indeed! Free of guilt and confusion and the tyranny of sin. At the moment I had a 100 percent loyalty to God, some sins that clung like barnacles, and a temporarily paralyzed spiritual condition. So I'd brought along my Bible and a small notebook filled with favorite quotations that I really wanted to think about. One of them read, "Jesus did not consider heaven a place to be desired while we were lost."—*The Ministry of Healing,* p. 105. Putting my head back against the seat, I thought about that one for a while as the harbors and bays slipped by beyond my window. That statement had more bound up in it than I could comprehend.

Don and I and our children live on a beautiful farm in western New York State. It is a place of lawns and trees, orchards and pines, a stream and a pond. We know our good fortune. But there have been times when one or another of our children was scrabbling for a foothold in the slippery business of growing up, that I couldn't see the beauty for my tears. Times when sunlight sheeting across the pond's ruffled surface meant nothing to me. Chrysanthemums, opening white and shaggy, could not heal the intensity of my suffering. Could it be that way with God over us? The truth is, we are a sorry lot.

The next quotation scribbled in my small notebook startled me out of generalities: "If but *one soul* would have accepted the gospel of His grace, Christ would, to save that one, have chosen His life of toil and humiliation and His death of shame."—*Ibid.*, p. 135. (Italics supplied.)

That idea staggers me. I do not know how to accept such love. It is very humbling.

Not long ago my friend Pat and I were taking part in the foot-washing ceremony that our church practices, and as she bathed my feet in warm water she said, "It isn't hard for me to do this for you—in fact, I have a good feeling about it. But it's hard for me to *accept* this service from you, or anyone else."

She had opened a door. With a flash of insight I realized that I felt the same way. Perhaps that had been the real issue on which Christ hoped to zero in. Hadn't that, after all, been Peter's problem ("Peter saith unto him, Thou shalt never wash my feet" [John 13:8])? And Christ said, "If I wash thee not, thou hast no part with me."

I had to learn how to accept the incomprehensible love and sacrifice of Jesus Christ—I, who knew a lot about giving, but not much about receiving. A concept, new and breathtakingly exciting, tiptoed around in my mind. It would not escape me forever. Now I had time and solitude in which to stalk it.

I look out the bus window. I watch my fellow passengers. I wonder where they are going and why. The frazzled young mother with two tiny tots. What destination could be worthy of what she is going through? A fragile, golden-haired 2-year-old whimpers on her shoulder as she spoons Gerber's carrots into the baby. Bus-weary, he doesn't really want food. Spitting out the orange mess, he cries. His mother mops up with a stained washcloth, stuffs everything into an over-flowing diaper bag, and tries, unsuccessfully, to comfort both children. Although tempted to offer my services, I feel the little ones are beyond responding to a stranger, so I watch with sympathy and am relieved for her when she gets off in a small town where a sensible-looking couple (who I assume are her parents) meet her.

An elderly man across the way reads *All the President's Men*. His badly deformed hands are stiff with arthritis, but his face is serene. He is enjoying this journey, and I realize I am, too. Or I had been until I consider where I am, that no one will meet me at the end of the line, and that I do not even have any real destination. The thing I am doing still appeals to me, however, even though foreboding vies with anticipation.

A girl wearing a classic brown sweater and lovely camel gauchos takes the seat beside me. Her skin is clear and her tawny hair long and shining. Suddenly I feel sad that youth is all behind me. That I am just a middle-aged woman (who doesn't feel middle-aged) in sneakers, sweatshirt, and jeans. She looks out the window during the stops in small towns and waves to people. This isn't foreign territory to her—it's home. Another sweater and skirt boards, and they discover each other. Realizing they are friends, I move so they can sit together. They notice me now. Thinking I'm an old dear who looks a bit stodgy like their moms, they thank me politely and settle down for girl talk.

We are nearing Rockland, that dot on the map that I

had circled weeks ago as the town in which I'd set off on foot. These are attractive, friendly towns. The kind I grew up in in Vermont, where everyone operates on a first-name basis. Warm greetings and farewells occur at every bus stop, much hollering across Main Street in good-natured banter. It's a marvelous atmosphere if one is part of it. But I know how the Yankee looks upon tourists. I grew up with the dry wit that fell from Yankee lips after a stranger's departure. Although I am one of them, they don't know it. They'd surely cock a skeptical eyebrow at my thirty years away. Gramp Kimball used to observe impatient motorists from the Empire State as they grew weary of the long lines of cars winding around narrow mountain roads. When they'd pull out and pass in spite of the danger, he'd say, "Watch them New York fools trying to commit suicide." Now I was one of the New York fools.

When we pulled into Rockland, I left the snug interior of the bus with reluctance. It was 3:30 P.M. The September sun was warm and penetrating. Wriggling into my bright-orange pack, I started walking. Passing a splendid two-story motel, I considered spending the night, delaying my leave-taking until morning, but suddenly I wanted to be off. Tomorrow could be no brighter nor more beckoning. Still, I didn't want to walk the distance to Camden that night. With a little luck I'd find a motel or two along the way.

Traffic in town was heavy and the road's shoulder narrow. Cars pulled out around me. It wasn't exactly how I had imagined it while poring over the map at home. The town seemed to stretch on forever—this *little* town. Slowly I began to unwind, to notice flower beds and children. I loved walking at home, but this was far better. Not knowing what was around the next bend, or what the next town would be like. Or even when I would arrive there.

It occurred to me that no one on earth knew exactly where I was. My husband would be busy in his office, wrestling with the demands of manufacturing. He'd miss me later when he got home, but right at this moment his mind was completely engrossed in the work he loved.

Our eldest daughter, Melody, married and living in San Francisco, didn't even know I was taking the journey. I had no idea what she'd think of my adventure. She's a sophisticated young woman, an attorney, wife of an attorney—yet she's a common gal, too, tuned to country people and their ways. Perhaps she'd look at me and shake her head. Or perhaps she'd be envious.

Kim, our Aleut and eldest son, living at home, would be out in the fields doing something with carrots or potatoes. He works at night as a security guard and as a part-time farm laborer by day. At 20 he's still poking at life with an exploratory finger. Now *he* might think of me as he hoisted crates in the fall sun. Although he didn't think my journey was a good idea, I had reminded him that just as he wanted freedom, so did I. We didn't argue, Kim and I. Our relationship can survive a lot of differing opinion.

Lori, our Korean daughter, our middle girl, also 20, would be contributing in her gentle way at the migrant workers' day-care center where she is employed. In between tucking little ones in for naps, she'd be planning the home supper menu. Without her I could not have come. It was she who would keep everything functioning smoothly, familiar foods upon the table, dust from off the floors. And she'd do it all without a word of complaint.

Jeff, also 20, also Korean, would be leaving the trade school he attends. But he would not give me a thought, for he's not the worrying kind. He keeps his own world right side up and assumes that others are able to do likewise. His confidence developed during his first six years when he had to live by his wits on the streets of Seoul. It has served him well.

Mitch, our 17-year-old son by birth, would be going about his business at the Christian boarding school that he attends eighty miles from home. He too had worried that my trip was a dangerous undertaking. Also he'd hinted that it would be nice if I'd stay home and tend to housewifely pursuits like other mothers. But he's a boy of strong and independent spirit himself, so I didn't feel greatly troubled about his reaction. Once I had heard him muttering about taking a solitary cross-country motorcycle trip. Undoubtedly I would have opportunity to pay my debt of worry. In the meantime I thought of him lovingly and wished he might see the ocean beneath its cloudless expanse of sky, for he always dismissed Maine as "too foggy for human habitation."

My thoughts came at last to our youngest, 13-year-old Amy. She would miss me, for as the older children had gone more and more about the business of life, I had had time for this daughter as I had not for the others. We were close. Too close, the other children said. "How would she go away to school when she had been Mom's little buddy so many years?" It was a good question, and I didn't have the answer. But one doesn't say, "Look, child, it's risky to love your mother too much. Run along." Yet somehow, when the shift from home to dormitory comes, I have the feeling she'll surprise us all.

Right now, as I hiked along Route 1, she'd be riding the bus between Rochester and Batavia, New York, on her own daily return from the school she attends. She wouldn't like the homecoming without me—I knew that. But her little dog, Hobo, would be there to welcome her joyously, and that would have to do.

The pedometer on which I had squandered $15 clicked away, but I had no confidence in it, for on a few trial runs at home it had proved disgustingly inaccurate. The road was a long gradual upgrade once it left the town. The weight of my pack began to be a burden. In the beginning I had said, "I'm going to strip this journey down to my Bible and a box of raisins." But, of course, it hadn't been that simple. Few things ever are. The little necessities kept piling up. One change of outer clothing, a rain poncho, lots of seemingly weightless underwear, toothpaste, shampoo, little packs of emergency food, an extra pair of sneakers, a notebook, and the Bible.

Amy had said, "Just take that tiny Bible Daddy had in the Army. Your Bible's way too heavy." Sensible advice I recognized.

But I had not heeded it. After the comfortable familiarity of my own worn, well-marked Bible, any other seemed an offense. Now I was paying for my decision. After I stopped to rest occasionally I noted that the slight breeze bit into my perspiring body even though the day was hot. Ten or fifteen minutes of resumed walking would then make me more comfortable. But I was more tired than I'd ever been hiking at home. Had fear of the unknown produced a wearying tension in my normally cooperative muscles?

Passing a couple motels, I debated whether or not to stop, and decided to go on. Surely there were more ahead. Through the treetops sloping downhill at my right I could see the ocean. In a way I felt cheated. I wanted it close enough to touch. But the world was lovely, fresh, and clean, tinged with the fragrance of spruce and the sea.

More motels. I really should stop. Had I come three miles or ten? Where would I eat? I had not seen as much as a McDonalds. Finally I decided I would walk ten more minutes. If no restaurant or further overnight accommodations appeared, I'd double back and stay in that neat white motel that sat well back from the highway.

Although I hated to admit it, I was exhausted. The road took on a desolate look. I explored around a couple more bends before turning back.

The genial host who came into the motel's office in response to the little bell on the door said, "You crept up on me. I didn't hear you drive in."

"That's because I walked in."

He glanced up from his desk, startled, really seeing me for the first time. "We don't get many hikers," he stated, looking me over cautiously, wary now.

"I'm just spending a few days walking along Route 1. Hope to get up to Belfast or Searsport." I tried to sound like the harmless housewife that I was.

The man relaxed. Now he only thought me crazy, not dangerous.

"I don't suppose there's a restaurant within walking distance, is there?" I asked hopefully.

"No, there's nothing closer than Camden, I'm afraid." Embarrassment tinged his voice. He felt somehow he'd failed as a host.

"It's not important," I replied. "I'm carrying a little food and won't go hungry."

"My wife and I are going into town later. Is there anything we can get for you?"

Instantly my independent nature asserted itself, but I thought then of the art of receiving that I'd pondered earlier on the bus. So I forced myself to say lightly, "A quart of milk would be a blessing, if you're sure it's no trouble."

"No trouble at all," he said, handing me the keys to my unit. "Though it may be an hour or two."

There was no busy harbor this night to entertain

me—only a small, neat room with a TV that didn't work. That was just as well, for I hadn't come to watch TV, though I did like to see the news.

It was a relief to slip the pack from my shoulders onto the twin bed. I have never liked motel rooms. No matter how thick the rug or luxurious the bedspreads, there's a lonely feel about them. Even with Don along I have felt it. I always long for the cozy clutter of our own bedroom at home.

Sitting down at the desk, I find motel stationery in the drawer and proceed to write to my good friend Nina. She does not even know I am doing this insane thing. (Later she will write, "What could you hope to see on foot that you couldn't have seen just as well from a car?" Oh, many things, my friend. Many, many things. There are compulsions one can't explain to even those nearest and dearest.)

But here now I find comfort in writing to her. It holds the strangeness of the room at bay. Why am I uncomfortable just because dusk is closing in? Couples and families walk by my window, chattering and laughing. A green station wagon turns into the drive, making my heart lurch, for it's an exact copy of ours at home—even to the luggage rack on top. But from the windows peer the faces of strangers. Children tumble out in restless relief, but they are not my children.

The season's last roses bloom in a small garden near my door and I am delighted with them. Flowers turn me on like angel dust. I often have the urge to weed and cultivate in gardens not my own. Just to give a little of myself to the flowers. These are like old friends, stumbled upon in a strange place. As I look at them a long time from my doorway, their glossy green leaves and scarlet petals strangely comfort me. It grows chilly. Closing the door, I go back to my letter.

I tell Nina what I am doing? It turns into a long

letter. After writing about our children, I ask about hers. I do not have to play any games with this friend. Long ago we shared all our frail mortality with each other. I can tell her that all my youthful dreams have not found fulfillment, and she will not think less of me. Or I can tell her I have ugly thoughts and she will not assume I have turned my back upon Christianity.

Years ago she and her minister husband drove into our yard one Sunday afternoon. Just assigned our church as their new pastorate, they were making some calls among the members. She wore a navy blue-dotted swiss dress with a white collar, and her dark hair was flipped at shoulder level. Nina was quick and bright and funny. Her husband was gentle, witty, and kind. We sat in our front yard enjoying the summer sun and the exploration of a new relationship. I think we all knew we had stumbled upon something good. When I went in to make lemonade, she tagged along. We talked. Eagerly, for all the years we'd missed. She was a swallow, darting, dipping, breaking the surface of my mountain lake calm. It's always been that way between us. In time they moved away, taking their nurturing to other congregations, but the friendship held. As often as possible we got together for Christmas and summer vacations. Our children became teenagers, and we prayed and struggled through those challenging years together. Of the hundreds who come and go in our lives, only occasionally do we stumble into such relationships where even miles and time cannot break the bonding.

Just as I finished the letter, the motel manager arrived at the door with a quart of milk. Once more I was aware of my own awkwardness when accepting a favor. He made a little milkman joke, and I thanked him profusely, probably too profusely, and when he left, I sat down to a paper cup of granola and milk.

I tried to write. That had been one of the purposes of

this journey. Rare, uninterrupted time to write. But it was hopeless. Ill at ease, I could not make friends with the unfamiliar room. I remembered one of our sons saying he could not study when he was homesick. Had his cozy dormitory room closed in upon him in this same way? But I was 49, not 16. This was ridiculous.

Finishing my granola, I wondered what to do with three fourths of a quart of milk. After a hot shower I crawled into bed. Lying there, I realized a noisy wind was whipping about in the treetops. I felt it blowing from the open window, sharp and cold, across my face. It sounded like a storm.

I tried to assess my day. There had been moments of pleasure, interspersed with panic, fatigue, and loneliness. Somehow I didn't care much for the inventory. I wanted to walk the earth with confidence. After all, this wasn't the ghetto. Actually I wasn't afraid of any external danger (although all my friends had gasped at my decision to come), only of my own inability to cope, my own untried strengths. A vague uneasiness had crawled into bed with me, but I never considered going home.

THE THIRD DAY

3 Woke to strong winds, a dark sky, and a very empty stomach. The milk, stored overnight in the window, tasted marvelous.

I dug a long-sleeved shirt out of my pack to wear under my hooded sweatshirt. Judging by the temperature of the room, I knew it would not be enough, but it was all I had.

Although I left the motel without a backward glance, I regarded with fondness the flowers along the drive. I would remember how they had looked in last evening's sunlight a long time.

It was only 8:00 A.M., and traffic was not yet heavy. The day before I had perspired. Now I shivered in a fierce wind that forced me to put up my hood and gather it tightly about my face. My legs, at first, were wobbly for lack of food.

But I was not unhappy. In fact, I could never remember experiencing such a heady mixture of freedom and anticipation. I had heard Camden, Maine, was the prettiest little town in America, and it was somewhere up ahead. All my apprehensions of the night before vanished as mysteriously as they had come. Within ten minutes I ceased to shiver, my legs no longer shook, and I grew accustomed to the weight of the pack. In that moment I knew I had made no mistake in coming, but rather that it would have been one to live out my years without ever doing anything alone in a faraway place. Without ever experiencing this wild, gray morning when I felt as strong as my 13-year-old, as wise as Eve, as daring as Wonder Woman.

An hour later, at the top of a long, steep rise, I removed my pack and sat down against a boulder to rest among the pines along the roadside. A stalk of Queen Anne's lace grew within reach. It is my favorite wildflower. I can never resist picking a blossom or two and studying its intricate design. All those minute flowerets opening one by one to create the whole. And that strange deep-purple dot in the center.

It occurred to me that my life was like that, a circle with God at its center. The circle signified my completeness in Him. I need not fear my life fragmenting, any more than I would expect the Queen Anne's lace to shatter away from its purple center. But if the flower was to realize its full beauty, it must blossom, floweret by floweret, from its perimeter inward. I had seen Queen Anne's lace that had opened delicately around their *outer* edges but failed to achieve full bloom. Then, I had also seen them big as saucers, with every tiny blossom fully open. A thing of startling beauty.

It was how I wanted my life to be, every facet of my being blossoming to the glory of God, but I knew I was more like the stunted blooms, flowering only on the outer edges. That's why I had come. For a long time I carried the flower with me as I hiked.

Finally I prayed, "Lord, let me start blossoming again, even if it's painful."

I thought about my first growth as a follower of Christ. It had come out of much reading, an immersing of myself in an eager spiritual search. Nothing else had mattered. My new friendship with Christ I had found more exciting than novels, movies, or television. Not a religious discipline, but a joy.

Then gradually so many things elbowed for space in my life. Children. Work. Hobbies. My career as a writer. As a speaker. I do not know when the balance shifted, but only that one day I realized much of the joy had slipped away and I was promoting to others a relationship that I had ceased to nurture or sometimes even to experience.

So I must make a decision. All matters of any importance demand decision. To recover my original experience, I must go back to the beginning and make a total commitment. It must be more than a pretty philosophy. Once more I would rise early to pray. That would necessitate going to bed earlier the night before, for I am not able to operate on five hours of sleep. Neither am I a person who enjoys retiring early. It is a discipline I have never mastered. Always one more letter to write, one more elusive line of poetry to create, one paragraph of prose, or, at the lowest extremity, one more half hour of ironing. Anything to stave off the humdrum buttoning down of the day. What is there about locking doors, adjusting thermostats, and brushing one's teeth that's so depressingly dull? I find even removing and hanging my clothing distasteful. All this preparation for six or seven hours of oblivion. My whole being rebels against it. But my husband reminds me that while I may be the arrogant queen of the night, I am also the battered victim of morning, and so, reluctantly, I drag myself off to bed, but always too late.

Now I must change if I am to recapture that which I have lost. Change involves more than one large decision. It consists of dozens of small ones, day by day. But if I'm to go on blossoming, ring by ring, toward my God-center, I must.

And there *are* compensations for the early-to-bed, early-to-rise routine. There's the wonder of standing before a window at dawn, speaking with the Creator while He's working with pink and gold along the black edges of night. If you've never experienced it, I can't tell you about it, and if you have, I don't need to. When man reaches out to Him hungrily, there's a magic between creature and Creator that contains the essence of Eden. For that's what Eden was all about, you know. Not eternal summer, though it was that, too, but God and man walking side by side, talking face to face, laughing at the same frolicsome chipmunk together. There by the window at dawn the experience comes close to the original. Why must I *discipline* myself to its delights? Part of me is so lonely for God—the other part so content with the familiar old rut in which I'm jostling around.

"O wretched man that I am! who shall deliver me from the body of this death?" (Rom. 7:24). You found your answers, Paul, or did you? Maybe you just hung on by sheer faith. Enough that God had the answers. I have read Romans 8 over and over seeking your conclusions, and your exuberant declaration at the end tells me you lived a jubilant life in Jesus Christ in spite of your "wretched man" outburst. "For I am convinced that neither death nor life, neither angels nor demons, neither the present nor the future, nor any powers, neither height nor depth, nor anything else in all creation, will be able to separate us from the love of God that is in Christ Jesus our Lord" (chap. 8:38, 39, N.I.V.).

After I'd walked along another mile or two spinning that Queen Anne's lace in one hand, I came upon a most unexpected little shop. From its windows lights twinkled, and it had about it an aura of Santa's workshop. I knew I was close to Camden and I had plenty of time. All day, in fact. Besides, I'm a Christmas nut and can get excited about holiday fixings in July.

Setting my pack just inside the door (I had visions of jostling an entire shelf of glassware onto the floor with that unaccustomed protuberance on my back), I strolled leisurely about the store. I had never heard of a Christmas shop before (was it open for business in the scorch of August?). Candles, cards, decorations, and gifts crowded the room. Knowing I could not add an ounce to my already-heavy pack, I walked about in frustration. Good discipline, I suppose.

When I set out once more, I knew my destination was not far ahead. Trudging along the outskirts of Camden, I thought that *discovery* was an exciting experience, whether it was the Pilgrims sighting the bleak Atlantic coast, Beethoven finding just the right note, or I entering this little Maine town. To *walk* into a town is totally different from whizzing through in a car. The first scattered houses alert the traveler that he has arrived. As the dwellings grow closer with an occasional business making its appearance, he experiences a kind of elation. His conquest of the road has earned him the right once more to mingle with his fellows.

Camden is cupped between the mountains and the sea, but one does not glimpse the latter at first. It would be quite possible to drive through Camden and never know one had come to water's edge, for the shops on Main Street obscure the harbor. But one senses something special about the place at first sight. Well-kept homes, window boxes showy with flowers, interesting shops and friendly people. I headed straight for an ordinary little restaurant—the kind where the locals sit on stools drinking coffee and making small talk. Taking a booth along the wall, I reveled in warmth, a place to stash my pack, and the smell of food. Nothing ever tasted better in my life than the oatmeal, toast, and hot chocolate I consumed. I thought as I sat there, trying to see through my steamy glasses, that it was a moment of total happiness.

With hunger appeased, I strolled up and down Main

Street, assessing the shops, knowing I'd fall prey to them later in the day. Then I wandered into a small park and found to my astonishment that the harbor lay before me. And Camden was, indeed, the prettiest little town in America. Sleek ships rocked on the choppy surface of the water, their tall sails flapping in the chill breeze. I know nothing of boats except that, like people, some are elegantly beautiful, some useful and plain. Camden's harbor, even under gray skies, was a thing to sit and admire, so I did just that. For a long time. It was inconceivable that I had no meals to prepare, no floors to sweep, not even any writing deadlines to meet. I was just sitting on a park bench by the sea, listening to the gulls, shivering a bit in the wind, and thinking there was no place on earth I would rather be at that moment.

As I looked at the backs of all those inviting little shops on Main Street I had myself a small chuckle, for the wind and sea had meddled with them over the years, and they were pretty scruffy.

After a while I took a tour of the town, partly to admire the neat New England architecture, partly to find a place to spend the night. The town was not overly blessed with sleeping facilities, but not too far from the downtown area I came upon an inn that appeared to have possibilities. Though well-kept, it was old, and would thus be free of the batik-bedspread syndrome that I found so depressing. Wistfully I looked up at the third-floor windows. Such a masthead view of the harbor would surely not be my good fortune, but I would settle for whatever was available. Those third-floor windows, framed in priscillas and huddling under the eaves, had a cozy look about them.

I should have known they'd be mine for the asking. Tourists aren't, after all, that plentiful in late September.

The proprietor, who had questioned my eccentricity

with his eyes, led me up the flights of stairs to my loft. The rooms glimpsed in passing displayed a homey blend of chintz and pine. My credit card had already whimpered at the cost of this carefully planned nostalgia, but I had no regrets.

My expensive little garret was simplicity itself. White chenille bedspread, white ruffled curtains, and a bath definitely of early origin. I loved it. Maybe I'd stay here forever. Well, at least for a few days. Closing the door behind me, I turned up the heat and stood at the windows a long time. One overlooked the bay; the other, the harbor and the town. A neighbor at home came from Camden. I imagined her as a little girl, running down the sidewalk below my window, not knowing that someday a sailor would come marching into her seaport town and into her heart, enticing her far away where no ships sailed to one's doorstep, and no mountains reared, blunt and rocky, at the back door. Had she been at ease with the sea, climbing into a rowboat as comfortably as city children mount bikes? Had she tuned her days to the coming and going of the tides? Was she now sometimes lonely for foggy nights and the monotonous clanging of the buoy in the bay? A practical, steady kind of woman, a good mother, a nurse, she doesn't seem to be. A proper New Englander, once she's made a decision, doesn't look back and pine for what she's left behind, but deep inside she's a New Englander forever. I'll bet Shirley thinks of the tall ships in the harbor sometimes when the hospital nights are long and quiet.

For thirty years I've been an uprooted Vermonter. While I love the small western New York town in which I live, the green Vermont valley where I grew to girlhood mocks the flat and fertile farmlands of my present home. My eyes are often lonely for dark mountains propped against the skyline. Sometimes in New York black cloud banks mass along the horizon, and I say to my youngest, "Pretend they're mountains. See how secure it feels to be protected by mountains." She squints her eyes and plays along with me, but she has no need for mountains—only for the lush and rolling countryside that has been her heritage.

I decide to wash my hair in the tiny corner sink. It is awkward, and I end up pouring the rinsewater with a drinking glass. Toweling my head before the mirror, I am amused at my situation. I have no rollers, nor do I plan to buy any. Neither do I plan to hunt up a hairdresser who will service unexpected customers. Instead, I'm simply going to comb, push into place, and hope for the best. My pretty little hairdresser back home assured me she had cut it in such a manner that all would be well. We had laughed then, knowing I didn't have the classic features for sleek little hairdos. But it really didn't matter, as she pointed out, for I'd not meet anyone I knew. To be truthful, I didn't even want to scare strangers, so I watched with trepidation as my fine brown hair dried and settled itself about my face. It was better than I had anticipated. A different me, but a passable one. Shaking my head from side to side, I let my hair swoosh about at will, then watched it fall neatly back into place with no help from comb or brush. A tremendous sense of freedom enveloped me. I could actually walk down the street without thought of wind or rain. In that moment I wished to be done with teasing and hair spray forever. Maybe I would be. Alongside my resolution to seek the Lord daily, I'd place another—to escape the tyranny of vanity.

Pulling a rocking chair up to the front window, I opened my Bible and knew a rare kind of peace. If problems had arisen at home, I didn't know about them. (At the moment my family had no way to find me, no matter what catastrophe befell them. That was a little scary.) I couldn't get over it—there was absolutely nothing I was supposed to be doing. If I wished, I could sit here and rock and read and look out at the sea all day. I could almost feel each nerve releasing its tension, amazed, like my hair, to be free.

With my Bible open on my knees to the book of Ezekiel, I read:

"A new heart also will I give you,

and a new spirit will I put within you" (Eze. 36:26).

That's what I wanted—a new heart. I had been praying for just that for months. There had been a time when I thought my old one was good enough—at least with a little cleaning up. But God had shown me that that was not the case. Those verses in Psalm 139 that read "Search me, O God, and know my heart: try me, and know my thoughts: and see if there be any wicked way in me" (verses 23, 24) were brave words on David's part. Inviting God to do a thorough scan of the heart requires courage, for I have learned that our hearts contain only spiritual refuse. I'm sure God showed David that hard fact gradually, as the psalmist was able to bear it. For it is unnerving to find that even one's apparent virtues often spring from wrong motives. Yet David was on the right track. We must be willing to let God view the whole ugly mess, and even worse, we must be willing to face it ourselves, then acknowledge our need of a re-creative act in our lives.

David ended his invitation to God humbly and wisely—"and lead me in the way everlasting" (verse 24). In other words he was telling God to clean house at any cost. Often I have wondered if I am willing to let God clean house with me, *at any cost*. For when God cleans house (or perhaps cleans heart would be a more appropriate term), *everything goes*. When one is born again, he is a new being, not a patched-up old one. That sounds exciting, but sometimes when God begins His work we find that parts of our old selves die hard.

Long-nurtured indulgences, little areas of ego, personality traits, comfortable but unproductive routines, private nooks of selfishness. How did I know? Because I'd been trying to let God do His work and found it painful. I fought against it. Ran from it. Here I was, even now, like Jonah, miles from home, and God was pursuing me yet. In this tiny room by the sea still saying, "A new heart also will I give you." Why am I intrigued by His offer, but afraid of the cost? Afraid of the pain. Afraid of submission.

Closing the Bible, I put my head back against the rocker. I wasn't sure I knew how to submit, to give up and let God do His work. People said religion was simple, but it wasn't. It was the most complex thing in the universe. Maybe the reason it was so sweet in my youth was because I'd never seen the whole canvas, only a little flower down in the corner.

I decided I would go shopping, forget eternal things and enjoy today. After tidying the room, I set out for town. In the back of my mind I already knew I'd succumb to a few purchases and mail them home. Something for the children—it was an old habit, not easily broken even now that they were grown. Seascape etchings for the girls, and tiny pewter sea gull tie tacks for the boys.

While browsing in a bookstore, hushed with an off-season shortage of customers, I grasped the opportunity to ask some questions.

What were the chances of finding motels ahead?

How about that fine line of a road on the map, the one that appeared to be at shore's edge?

The proprietor was friendly and interested in my venture. Yes, there were motels ahead, though perhaps too widely spaced for a walker.

That charming little road by the sea was privately owned, and offered no haven to the traveler afoot. Best cross it off my agenda.

As I left the store, I noted dark clouds gathering. A strong wind hurled the dust of the street, and the first raindrops, upon those stragglers who had not heeded the storm's early warnings.

The man at the store had recommended a tiny eating place called Yorkies. Racing along Main Street, I turned right, turned right again, and there it was, a welcome haven in a lonely town on a stormy night. That nourishing breakfast now seemed far behind me. The bookstore proprietor had informed me that Yorkies' waiting line sometimes reached the sidewalk at the peak of tourist season, but on this bleak September evening it was only cozily crowded. I found a small corner table.

Fifteen minutes later a steaming bowl of corn chowder sat before me, flanked by a tossed salad and two large blueberry muffins. Simple food prepared with creativity and expertise. No wonder the tourists stood in line. Dreading the little garret room that had appeared so inviting in the light of day, I lingered long in the warmth of the place. Finally, having no excuse to dawdle longer, I paid my bill and ventured into the dark street. The men in the restaurant said it was a nor'easter. So here I was at ocean's edge with one of those famous storms lashing the harbor into whiteness. It was exciting, especially so since I didn't have to huddle under a rain bonnet but could let my hair blow in the wind like the teenagers who still lingered on the streets. The route to the inn provided a clear view of the bay, and in the last light of day it was an awesome sight with great waves piling up against the rocky shore. The darkness was ominous, and I wished for friends and a welcoming hearth. But I had come for aloneness, and that's what I was experiencing.

Pausing a bit in the wind and rain at the top of the

hill, I attempted to absorb the essence of the moment. Never before had I realized how dependent we are upon familiar faces, voices, surroundings. I had often felt a tinge of the same loneliness when traveling in some far place with my husband, but comfort had been as close as his arms. That is quite different from standing alone in the darkness in a strange town at the edge of the crashing sea. This isolation, however, was of short duration and of my own choosing.

What of John on the Isle of Patmos?

Of prisoners of war in solitary confinement?

Or a 2-year-old deposited with an unknown baby-sitter in a strange household? My friends at home had asked, "Why are you doing this crazy thing? I would not enjoy it alone."

But I had to know what *alone* felt like, to discover whether or not I could endure it, even briefly. Not alone like going for a walk at home, or being by oneself in the house when husband and children are at school and work. That's a comfortable, familiar isolation. But *alone* where you have no one to turn to and no beckoning lights of home. Now that's a different matter.

Who was I, apart from husband, children, and friends? What inner resources were mine? Had I retained any connection with the child of long ago who had so often felt alone even among familiar settings? Was I a *person* other than the faithful wife, devoted mother, and active participant in my church?

I had made a lot of choices during my forty-nine years and they had molded me into the individual I now was. Sometimes I had grown weary of her. Weary of her pleasant conformity. Weary of the strings that bound her like invisible umbilical cords to other people.

June, the wife.

June, the mother.

June, the teacher.

June, the listener.

June, the friend.

June, the writer.

June, the dedicated Christian.

Most of the time I had loved those roles. Now and then I had resented them. Some had hurt too much. Others had demanded too much. Several had cast me as better than I really was, leaving me fearful and exhausted as I struggled to maintain the image.

I was Max Kimball's daughter, thus often too easygoing for my own good. Not excelling in self-discipline. But I had his sense of humor, too. Sometimes the world and its occupants seemed uproariously funny to me. Witty words rose to my lips and I suppressed them because they did not fit the image—or maybe just because life had become dead serious, leaving no room for wit.

Maybe I wanted only to be a child again.

Against the rules.

No going back.

Was I Alice Kimball's daughter too? Perhaps all my life I'd sought that part of myself inherited from a 19-year-old girl I'd never known. One whose life I'd destroyed with my own birth. A heavy knowledge to carry through the years. I suppose it was she who had brought me to this place, for during her brief alighting among the Vermont hills she had written whimsical poetry and dabbled watercolors onto paper in lovely ways. A seeking, sensitive, creative woman, her contribution to my genes had driven me down many a strange road. Helped me enjoy one autumn leaf rather than racing around gathering great handfuls. Gifted me with a kind of loneliness that was both sweet and painful. Yes, I was her daughter too. A unique blending of two people, as we all are. Or maybe I was no longer unique. Some days I felt like a carbon copy of the proper middle-aged woman of the late twentieth century.

Was I here to break out of that mold? To regain my uniqueness? Sometimes we lose it after walking down so many ordinary roads. Life demands a *lot* of ordinary roads, yet I've noticed those who shun them often end up in a bramble patch. The trick is to accept them, all the while maintaining one's individuality. How? I'm not quite sure. Certainly one does not sink to watching soap operas, or washing windows whether they need it or not. One must keep blossoming toward his or her God-center, like the Queen Anne's lace. Learning, changing, growing, giving, and daring to be oneself, but always with love. Many, in an attempt to guard their vulnerable selves, have trampled all over those about them. I've been guilty too. Jesus Christ was the most unique being ever to set foot on this planet, yet He was gentle with people without compromising His individuality in any way. In fact, that's what set Him apart. He dared to be selfless in a selfish world. To meet the dusk without knowing where He was going to sleep, and to let dawn discover Him on His knees in some remote and lonely place. Jesus was comfortable with earth-life in a way that we have never learned. Maybe because He never compromised or played games or worried about His image. Or maybe because He knew no path that led beyond His Father's will. With the crescendo of the storm building all about me, here at the side of the sea, I longed for that sure, settled, single-minded approach to living.

Climbing the porch steps, I tugged open the heavy door and snuggled into the welcoming cheeriness of the lobby. A middle-aged couple sat before a blazing fire chatting. At my entrance they looked up, smiled, and invited me to join them. They were at home here, having vacationed in Camden for years. Eagerly they told me of the sailing ships that traveled between

A LITTLE JOURNEY

Camden and Boston, of the trails in the hills behind the town. The fact that I was wandering about alone quite astonished them. That, and my rather bedraggled appearance from too much philosophizing in the rain, probably provided their topic of conversation when I later climbed the stairs. But they were charming and said they envied me a bit.

I wasn't quite sure why I chose to leave the hearth and their pleasant company. Perhaps because, as a temporary single person, I didn't know how to relate to a couple. For so many years I'd been part of a twosome. During a moment of panic I glimpsed the wilderness of widowhood. It is awkward to be alone in social situations. Oh, I'd read about it, of course, but never experienced it. I wondered how I'd manage if it ever happened to me. Now I understood the groups of older women playing cards, eating out, and taking Sunday afternoon rides (how silly I'd thought they looked in their blue hair and church hats). A make-do life in a manless world. Better than sitting home and chasing memories in the butterfly nets of nostalgia, but I wouldn't like it. No, not at all.

Rain hurled itself against the small-paned windows, while wind whispered old sea tales under the sash. This night was better than the last. I was not relaxed enough to write, but at least I could now read. Maybe I was catching the rhythm of this journey after all. Climbing between the virgin sheets, I wondered, Had I no money, could I find a job and survive? I knew all about frugality. My husband had taught me that in the very beginning when it was nip and tuck financially. And I had become extremely good at it. Sometimes these days I miss the challenge of budgeting. I marvel that some of my children have never bothered to learn the art of making ends meet, watching a bank account grow, and seeking out the perfect little gift with a wee price tag. But it didn't really matter about the job-hunting and survival, for I was knee-deep in credit cards and traveler's checks. Rather I had only to find wealth of mind and soul. Over the past couple of days I had carried a possible source upon my back long enough to have increased its value appreciably. From my pack, I dug out my dog-earned old Bible and turned to the twenty-second psalm. I had stumbled upon it once long before and read in utter amazement David's prophecy of his Lord's death on the cross. Had he known, that harp-strumming young monarch of Israel, the tragic moment he foretold?

> I read fragments, like poetry, against the storm.
> My God, my God, why hast thou forsaken me?
> All they that see me laugh me to scorn.
> I am poured out like water.
> My strength is dried up like a potsherd.
> My tongue cleaveth to my jaws.
> Thou hast brought me into the dust of death.
> The assembly of the wicked have enclosed me.
> They pierced my hands and my feet.
> They part my garments among them, and cast lots
>   upon my vesture.
> But be not thou far from me, O Lord.
> O my strength, haste thee to help me.

Turning out the light, I felt the raw, lonely humanity in those words. I tried to comprehend that He had done it for me. That death should no longer be my heritage. That I might lie down in peace whether at home, in the bosom of my family, or alone in a strange town on a stormy shore.

Tonight I understood a little more about loneliness. I was hundreds of miles from home. He had been light-years from His, with only the credit card of faith in a Father who eventually put Him to the test. ("My God, my God, why hast thou forsaken me?") Yet for you and me, and any other receptive human, He had held on, taking such comfort as He could find from the scanty friendship of earthlings and from those sunrise talks with His Father.

As high winds shook the inn and caused my bed to tremble, I wondered why it is we take Christ's astonishing visit to our planet so complacently. I expect other inhabitants of the universe marvel at both His act of love (at first I wrote condescension, but that's not the right word, is it?), and our unpardonable indifference. At that moment I felt very close to Him. Maybe only when we have stripped away familiar sustaining relationships, and our secure environment, can we glimpse the abyss between heaven and earth, and the loving and lonely dynamics He practiced to bridge it.

Sleep took me captive despite the wind, which hurled waves noisily across the harbor. It occurred to me, as I drifted drowsily toward oblivion, that the inhabitants of Camden were probably not in the least disturbed by the weather or the contemplative stranger in their midst.

Hours later I woke to a persistent pounding. In the blackness of the stormy night it was an eerie sound. And it went on and on. Obviously someone was trying to get in the side entrance of the hotel. Why? I squinted my farsighted eyes at the feebly glowing hands of my watch. No use. A fumbling for glasses. Two o'clock in the morning. Where was the innkeeper? Was I the only person in this mansion of yesteryear? How had it looked so quaint and charming in the morning light? It was turning into the kind of tale I never watch on television.

Getting up, I peeked into the hall. There had to be a few other guests. What about the couple I'd chatted with at the fireside? Was everyone sleeping through this strange intrusion of our rest, or was I having some kind of private nightmare? The loud thumps continued steadily into the stillness, now and then punctuated with a rattling of the doorknob. Certainly no one of evil intent would be making so much noise, so why was my heart pounding?

Had someone seen flames and come to report a fire? Sniffing for smoke, I tried not to think of the long stairway winding to my attic hideaway. Surely there was a fire escape. There were laws about such things.

When I had just about decided to go out into the small hallway and yell, "Whoever's in charge here, there's someone at the door," a young man blundered sleepily toward the stairway, then made his way to the first floor and the source of the pounding. Shamelessly I eavesdropped. After all, I was part of this drama.

The young man wrenched the door open, and a bedraggled middle-aged couple dripped into the lighted lobby.

"How could you lock us out in such weather?" The woman's voice was strident, her words slightly slurred. Obviously, they'd found some nightlife, even in this remote spot.

The young man played the gracious host in that comic setting with such proper formality that I longed to applaud from my balcony seat. "The door is never locked, madam. It simply swells a bit in a storm and requires a little extra strength to open it. Just a gentle shove with your shoulder would have done the trick. I am sorry you were inconvenienced."

"We've been pounding for at least fifteen minutes," the woman grumbled as they plodded moistly up the carpeted stairs. The young man, squishing barefoot in their wake, muttered apologies. As he passed my door moments later I could not read the expression on his face (you must remember I was peeking through an extremely small crack). I still don't know why he chose the third floor from which to guard the inn. Perhaps he'd had too many knockings in the night.

Crawling back into bed, I expected to lie awake till dawn, the supercharged victim of all that adrenaline, but maybe I'm better at handling suspense than I'd suspected, for I dropped off to a delicious sleep and woke at nine the next morning to gray light and the drumming of rain. The nor'easter had settled in with no concern for my itinerary.

THE FOURTH DAY

4 Though my pack contained a poncho purchased for just such days, I dreaded setting out in the downpour. I lay in bed soaking up the luxury that was mine. A warm and cozy room, no particular place I had to go, and the pleasant fury of the storm drenching my windowpanes. I loved storms. It was a gift my grandmother gave me when I was growing up in her home during the thirties. When thunder rolled down our valley and lightning flickered over the wooded hillsides, Gram turned the telephone's mouthpiece away from the living quarters, shut all windows to avoid drafts, which she said attracted lightning, and herded me onto our long open front porch, where we settled ourselves to watch the fireworks. Such is the power of childhood influence that to this day I have little sympathy for people who fret, and dogs who huddle under beds, when thunder rolls. We once had a collie who raced wildly about outside during electrical storms, barking at the heavens, nearly frantic with fear. At least she dealt with the problem head-on. That I could admire.

Finally I reached for an apple on the bedside stand, a perfect Red Delicious I'd picked up at a corner grocery on the way into town the morning before. That and a small package of almonds would make a fair breakfast. Propping myself up against the pillows, I thought about the strings that dangle from our lives back into the mists of infancy and childhood. What was my very first memory? Many times I had tracked it stealthfully. Such an elusive thing, a first memory. Yet my sleuthing always took me to the exact same moment of time. I am behind a large flour barrel in my grandmother's pantry and someone is screaming at me. It is not my grandmother, for she didn't scream, and had she been there, I would not have experienced the terror that clamps around my heart even today as I hold myself to the memory. It must have been some girl hired to take care of me while my grandmother taught school. What had I done to incur her wrath? What was she saying? I can never hear the words. But I can feel the helpless fear, and the cringing. There were no blows, only the words flailing me and the angry nameless face above me. Even today I cannot stand the anguished face of a little child as the harsh words of an adult pelt into him. The stomach-knotting fear of my flour-barrel refuge lives again, fresh as yesterday, and I long to gather the little one into my arms. It may have made me too gentle a mother. I do not know. Childish mistakes mattered little to me—spilled milk, torn clothing, broken dishes—but I was fierce about moral matters. Dishonesty of any kind.

One of our sons once borrowed, without asking, a tool from a man who used our barn to stable his horses. In his unskilled, little-boy hands it broke. He came to me in horror. Now what? I told him the tool must be returned with ample money to replace it.

"I can't do that," he said, tears welling.

"I will go with you," I assured.

"I still can't."

"There is no other way. He will understand. You will see." Feeling his fear, I fought the urge to spare him.

Dutifully he emptied money from his bank, and we

went together toward the place of restitution. I don't know which of us hurt the more. The kindly man heard the almost inaudible confession with compassion. Even yet I can still see him bending on the newly spread hay of the horse stall in the dimly lit barn, looking into the child's tear-stained face.

"Son, I've got another of those gadgets at home," he said, "and I can't take your money, but I admire your courage. And let's consider that toolbox our joint property from now on."

So what did he learn, our son, from that frightening confrontation? That we must deal with our errors head-on, no matter how much it goes against the grain? That his usually easy-going mother was positively flinty when a moral issue was involved, and that humanity is surprisingly compassionate when we humble ourselves to confession? I cannot be sure he learned those lessons, but at least they are the ones I sought to teach.

As a youth I was not scrupulously honest. No, I never went shoplifting. It wasn't in vogue at the time. But I thought nothing of snacking in the home of a woman for whom I did ironing. And if a small, or even a large, deceit would comfortably cover a misdemeanor, I counted myself both fortunate and clever. It was a few years later, when I caught a glimpse of the absolute integrity of Christ, that I saw the ugliness of dishonesty even in its most acceptable forms. Insofar as I was able, I made right the errors of the past. Some of the restitutions were most embarrassing. Knocking on the door of a former employer, I told him I'd mailed a lot of personal letters out of the company stamp drawer. I didn't know how many, but I gave him more than enough money to cover them. He was astonished. At a total loss for words. Finally he said he expected every secretary had done the same. Business firms allowed for such things. Some years later, when I needed a recommendation, he wrote my prospective employer that I was a person of "the utmost integrity." Not really, sir. Just one who'd seen herself standing grubby and earthbound in the shadow of her Lord.

Rain continued to fall beyond my window—on the sea, on the mountains, on the boats in the harbor, on the people scuttling along wet streets. Sodden leaves hugged the gutters. Making my bed with its Victorian white coverlet, I decided to stay on another day rather than brave the elements. That was a mistake. From that point, my emotions began to mirror the gray mists of the fog and drizzle outside. I had not come to hibernate (though there had been moments at home when hibernation sounded just two stops short of paradise), and I should have kept moving.

The day before, I had acquired a cardboard box from an obliging storekeeper and now proceeded to pack the small gifts I'd purchased for the family. To them I added my second set of sneakers. Expensive ones, purchased for this very trip, they had proved less comfortable than the old "cheapies" I'd worn for several years and brought along only for an emergency. Much as I hated to admit it, my pack was heavy—not impossibly so, but uncomfortably so. Putting my dirty laundry into a plastic bag and using it for stuffing, I taped and labeled the box. It awaited only its trip to the post office on the morrow.

I, who had longed for solitude in which to read and write, could do neither. Although I had written entire books amid the confusion and interruptions of a large family, I could not deal with this strange, quiet room even though the sea lapped at my doorstep and I was snug as a kitten on a hearth. Was it possible I had to have familiar surroundings? I did not think so, for I had written reams in far places while traveling with Don, drawing inspiration from everything about me. Then it meant I had to have *familiar people*. I fought against that. Dependency. I feared it.

At last I decided I would go downtown. Confined in this tiny room too long, I felt it closing in on me. The fresh air was a tonic, but the town no longer interested me. I had seen its curios, browsed in its bookstore, wandered its side streets. However, I needed a clean shirt, a long-sleeved one, for the dampness was moving into my marrow. The clothing in the shops was surprisingly chic and expensive, geared to tourists. I narrowed my selection to two turtleneck knit shirts— one a soft blue, the other bright-red. Blue was my color—I had a closet full of that very shade at home—but I took the red. I wasn't June Strong who wore the blue that matched her eyes—I was someone else. Or I hoped I was. It hit me then that maybe we are all only the person we have become in relation to others, and I had no relationships at the moment against which to define myself. Except my relationship with God. He was here with me in Camden, Maine. That I knew. I wasn't sure, however, that I knew how to relate to Him when I was shorn of all earthly relationships. Perhaps, I feared, I took the measure of my friendship with Him by my success, or lack of it, as a mother, wife, neighbor, writer, et cetera. Now I was alone, with a new red shirt and a very hazy concept of who I was. And God was observing.

Here in this seaside hamlet I sought the young woman I had once been. I hoped her essence still existed within the complex creature I had become. She had had more independence. I liked her better. The older woman seemed weak and vulnerable. Perhaps she was life-scarred and wise. Or perhaps she had learned that no matter how jauntily one steps out into life at 20, there could be trauma, challenge, disappointment, pain. And one must cope. In the coping one changes. One accepts that he or she cannot meet every challenge. Failure is possible. Those one loves may, knowingly or unknowingly, cause pain. In the process one gives away an unbelievable amount of one's self.

This lady, this middle-aged gal I didn't much care for—had she lost the fierce independence of youth? Did it matter? Would she discover a clearly defined self apart from the debris of living through which she'd fought her way? Would what she discovered have any bearing on her battered friendship with God? Was it possible that humanity must submit to a humbling process to be part of the heavenly family? Could the initial arrogance be our natural inheritance from our father the devil? Was the thing she sought best left behind? Was she, after all, really *supposed* to be anyone apart from this conglomerate she'd become? Was she the *real* June Strong? I'd wear the red shirt anyway. Let it represent a badge of survival—or maybe of growth.

In the evening I wandered once again through the rain to Yorkies and ordered vegetable soup and bran muffins. I was glad for light and warmth, and most of all for people, those marvelous creatures who laugh and talk and touch. Not that they spoke to me. But the place was alive with small-town togetherness, and that was the best I could hope for under the circumstances. I recalled lines from Siegfried Sassoon's poem "Alone":

"I thought of age, and loneliness, and change.
I thought how strange we grow when we're alone,
And how unlike the selves that meet and talk,
And blow the candles out, and say goodnight."

I had always thought it an excellent poem, the words depicting a universal experience with a lovely honed brevity, as all good poetry must. But now I *felt* the poet's words deep within as something more than a well-plied art form. What did *I* really know of loneliness, playing games here by the sea? What of the elderly woman I knew at home? Husband dead, children indifferent. Friends too busy. Just getting out of her wheelchair and into bed, she'd told me, took nearly thirty minutes every night, and the danger of falling as she maneuvered with one hand—the other was gnarled beyond usefulness with arthritis—was a very real possibility. And we let people live like that, tossing them a bone of companionship now and then when it's convenient, because we never really understand what it's like until we're there ourselves and then it's too late.

Even the teenager struggling out of his adolescent cocoon can be pretty lonely right in the heart of his own family.

*   *   *   *   *

The nor'easter was abating. As I left the restaurant, the horizon was a deep cobalt blue, behind small, paler blue clouds. I wanted to be content in this place. I wanted to look out the window and know it as a familiar beauty, like the hilltop cornfield behind our home where sunlight gilds a rustling ballet of leaf and stalk at dusk. That New York sky is the same cobalt blue. Its shades and variations I know intimately, but I cannot make this ocean-sky horizon my friend. I can only see its loveliness in a detached analytical way.

Back in my room, I make a decision.

I will go home.

The instant it is made, I feel better. Unpacking the box I had prepared for mailing, I stuff everything, even the gifts, into my backpack. No burden is too heavy on the way home. The awful truth assails me.

I am bitterly lonely. I am not functioning well at all. My experiment has failed. I am only an extension of my limited community after all. Cut off, I bleed and die.

As I sit in the rocking chair by the window I

experience a curious peace. The slate-blue clouds mound like hills against the deeper blue, while waves foam shoreward from far places. An occasional small boat speeds into the harbor, halts briefly, then arcs about, heading seaward again, at one with the stormy elements. Although I have traveled far to be in this place, I am not a part of it. I will never be. Even if I were to move here I would be a tourist ten years hence. Had I gone to that corner of Vermont where I know every curve of the land, every towering spruce, I suspect it would have made no difference. I'd have succumbed to loneliness. For even that beautiful spot is no longer home. Through hard experience I have learned that going back to my beginnings only makes me infinitely sad. Too many memories. Too many rooms where strangers dwell. Too many paths that no longer know the shape of my foot. Maybe Thomas Wolfe was right. Maybe we can't go home again.

The earth, however lovely, is not a friend. It saddens me to learn that. She has nurtured and comforted me always, but I now know that is ineffective without the balancing nurture of people, ideally family. When I'd walked the familiar woods at home, I'd sometimes held private praise sessions, telling God how great He'd been to me in various areas of my life. Invariably I'd thank Him first for the out-of-doors and the aesthetic pleasure I gained from it. But now I have learned, in four restless days, that surf and sunsets cannot take the place of voices and laughter. Yet so often in the very midst of banter and togetherness, I'd longed for an isolated beach. Perhaps man ever seeks a balance between the two.

I'd been so sure this journey would effect a change in my life. For years I'd thought If I could only be *alone,* even for a few days. If I could just sit down by the ocean somewhere and *think,* surely I could decide what life was about before it was all over. And here I was, but the earth had failed me. She had no answers. As always, she was exquisitely beautiful, but that was all. I'd not found my solutions in the heart of my family or alone with the wind and the sea. I couldn't even define the questions, much less the answers.

Crawling into bed, I opened my Bible to the beginning of the first chapter of the book of John. Those joyous verses (1-4) tell us that Christ was *Life* and that *Life* was the *light of men*. Or at least it was meant to be, but verse 5 is a sad commentary on the actual facts—"And the light shineth in darkness; and the darkness comprehended it not." Talk about lonely assignments! I tried to picture Christ, the Prince of heaven, laying aside His royal garments and preparing for exile on Planet Earth, bringing with Him healing for every man's need. He must have experienced moments, perhaps hours, of struggle as He separated Himself from the adoration of angels and the fierce filial love of His Father and descended into the bleakness of sin. Into that place where death always has the last word. But He brought life, and that life was the only hope the citizens of Planet Earth would ever have. No science fiction could possibly compare with that drama.

I expect He too had the option to turn back at any time. What had held *Him* when the nights were bleak and lonely?

Love.

Only love.

Well, my venture had no noble purpose, and its defeat would cause no loss. My family, chuckling a bit, would rejoice that Mom was home to feed the troops and oversee the laundry. ("Let's hope she got whatever it was out of her system.") Robbed now of even that beckoning dream in which I fancied myself scribbling prolifically upon some rock-strewn shore, I would fight to find a spare hour here or there in which to write.

It was a little sad and a little funny. I was glad I at least knew it was a little funny.

Just as I was drifting off to sleep, a thought flitted, like Pac Man, across my mind. Yes, I had sought answers in my relationships with the human family, had sought them here in isolation, but it was *Christ* who was the Light of men. I was seeking in the wrong places. Had I known Him so long, yet somehow missed the very heart of what He longed to share with me? I had always felt faint contempt for those who "received him not." How could anyone reject my Lord? What blindness robbed the Jews of their Messiah?

Yet I, who had known the Lord for thirty years, slept here on an unfamiliar shore because I was disoriented in the universe. Right within the bright warmth of His glory, I was confused and stumbling. No better than those who'd asked, "Can any good thing come out of Nazareth?"

I've walked with You thirty years, Lord. Why do I still have questions?

Canst thou by searching find out God? (Job 11:7).

I've felt your presence working in my life over and over again. Why have You stuck with me when I have comprehended so little?

The mountains shall depart, and the hills be removed; but my kindness shall not depart from thee, neither shall the covenant of my peace be removed, saith the Lord that hath mercy on thee (Isa. 54:10).

Then our original commitment is still valid, even though I've desecrated its lofty principles many times? Often I've felt so cut off from You as a result of my sins.

Fear not: for I have redeemed thee, I have called thee by thy name; thou art mine (chap. 43:1).

Such love is beyond my understanding. When I truly

know You, my Lord, I expect I shall, at last, know myself also. I long for that enlightening.

Ye shall seek me, and find me, when ye shall search for me with all your heart (Jer. 29:13).

Perhaps I had not come in vain after all.

THE FIFTH DAY

5 Good, bright, after-the-storm sunlight spilled across the bed, demanding attention. As I swung my legs over the side and surveyed the morning sleepily the little room took on its original tidy charm. My bulging pack on the straight-backed chair spoke stolidly of last night's defeat. What had ever made me think I could carry such a hulk even to the bus stop?

Reaching for my glasses to focus the day, I crouched before the window. The morning was alive with gulls and sun-dusted whitecaps. *And I knew I would go on. Nothing could have stopped me.*

Sheepishly I emptied my pack of all the extras and once more prepared the parcel for mailing home, grateful I'd bought a generous supply of strapping tape. The innkeeper eyed me curiously as I Master-Charged my exit, but a paying customer had her rights to eccentricity, and he bade me a safe journey.

The world was washed and glittering, no kin to yesterday's gray phantom. Descending the hill into town, past the *Down East Magazine*'s headquarters, whose windowboxes hung bright with color, I knew a heady anticipation that could have taken me around the world. As I deposited my parcel at the post office I thought how close I had come to turning back. My time was running out. Whatever I was to learn on this journey must be revealed soon.

Entering the same little restaurant where I'd breakfasted upon my arrival in Camden, I took a stool at the counter. While I fortified myself with hot oatmeal and orange juice, the waitress packed me a lunch for the road. A young woman sitting directly behind me in a booth watched with interest as I wiggled into my pack's bright orange straps.

"You hiking?" she asked shyly.

"Just for a few days." I felt a little foolish about the whole production.

"I think that's great. I wish I had the courage to set out and do something on my own, but my family'd think I'd gone mad."

"Sometimes you have to risk that," I said, zipping my sweatshirt and grinning down at her.

"Maybe someday I will. Good luck, ma'am, and be careful. There's some tough customers on the road these days."

That's what my family had feared, the "tough customers." So far I hadn't seen any, unless you counted the doubts and fears that had danced round my room the night before. Thanking her, I headed out.

It was the best walking I'd done, as though last night's struggle and defeat had possessed some purging power. Rounding the bend out of town, I breathed deeply of the pine-scented air. I was 100 percent gypsy. Huge trucks barreled by, nearly sucking me off my feet with the blast of their passing. But it was too early for much traffic. Mostly I was alone. Absolutely alone with the wind and the pines and the clear blue sky. Cut off from the past and the future. This week stood like a hyphen between my long years of mothering and whatever lay ahead. Maybe I was scared of the future. Of being 50 and then 60 and then . . . old. Until now I hadn't had much time to think about it. I'd been too busy tying up the loose ends of child-raising, writing, washing jeans, and cooking oversized casseroles. At home, whizzing frantically through my days, getting old didn't seem all that bad. Sort of restful. That was part of my problem. I was tired, just plain physically tired, from running as fast as I could for twenty years. But I had no one to blame except myself.

From the time the first baby entered our home I'd felt the children could never thrive in my absence. On rare occasions I'd entrusted them to my mother-in-law (in whom I'd had total confidence, but upon whom I'd not wished to impose), but no teenager, no stranger, ever assumed the responsibility of child care in our home. That was a mistake. It hurt our marriage. It hurt the children. And it hurt me. All those years Don and I rarely had a day or a weekend alone together. As the children grew older we didn't even have an evening by ourselves. Absorbed in child-rearing, I felt no lack, but Don did. I now know one does not have the right to do that to a marriage partner. It's to Don's credit that our relationship survived in spite of my obsession with motherhood.

Neither does such concentrated mothering enrich children. To the contrary, it produces shy youngsters who tend to be homesick at summer camp or away from home. They make their adjustment, of course, but in the meantime they suffer needlessly. A good baby-sitter occasionally not only breathes a little romance back into the marriage but exposes the child to a different type of care. He learns he can put on his own T-shirt even if it *is* backward, and that the sun will come up in the morning even if his mom isn't there to tuck him in at night.

I was still all for mothering—too much is far less serious than too little—but I also knew I was walking that Maine highway partly because I'd overplayed my act. Somewhere along the way I'd lost contact with the person I'd been "before children." When they were small, their needs and dependence justified the hard work. Then I didn't mind long hours. They paid me in hugs and assurances of love. Now, as young adults they didn't really need me. They were becoming well integrated into their own worlds, but the laundry and the cooking and the long days were still with me. I liked the people they were becoming—their lighthearted views on everything taking place about them. But physically I was weary. Not so willing to race from dawn till bedtime anymore. Maybe that time comes for every mother, or maybe I was just too eager to get on with my own future. I'd always labeled myself home-maker and joyed in the role. Only lately had the word *servant* popped into my mind. A household of adults had elected me to wash clothes and scrub floors while the rest went about activities of their own choosing.

Somehow I'd lost my reasons for everything. When-ever I wanted to write, dishes needed doing. And when I needed to meet distant speaking engagements, some-one else's schedule got in the way. And some days I felt annoyed with everyone.

It occurred to me, walking along that shore road, that I was angry most of all with the children for *growing up*. I'd liked mothering. Better than the early days of secretarial work at which I'd been reasonably efficient, and even better than this writing business, which was new and exciting. I liked the lazy summers when the screen door banged all day, and the children thought making popcorn and fresh spearmint tea on the outdoor fireplace a big event. I liked too snowy Sunday nights when we read books around the fire and the weighty matters of the world were nothing to us, because we were safe and secure and together.

And I liked the closets full of little girls' dresses and

the wonderful clutter of wires and tools and solitary socks in the boys' rooms. With amusement I'd read of women who couldn't handle the loss of their children. Well, most of mine hadn't really gone anywhere yet, physically at least. But they were already departed in spirit, and the literal exodus would soon follow. Now I wanted it all back. Simple and uncomplicated. It wasn't really the work I resented these days, I realized with a lump in my throat; it was the ending of something that could never be the same again. And no one had asked me if it was OK, even after the tremendous investment I'd made. An emotional investment, and that's the worst kind. During a rather bittersweet childhood I'd decided not to get too deeply involved with anyone throughout the remainder of my life. Just to play it safe, so goodbyes were never painful. But somehow the children had invaded my resolution and exposed me to hurt.

My paternal grandmother who'd moved, without whimpering, into the maternal role in my life after my mother's death stayed with me till my sixteenth year. Then she, too, took her place in the hillside cemetery. I hate gravestones. They were the chapter headings of my childhood. I shed no tears at my grandmother's death—I was beyond tears. Instead I went back to boarding school and made merry with my already too-merry friends. I would not let whatever evil force was pursuing me catch up and destroy me. Young and well, I would choose to sorrow, or not to sorrow. And I chose not to.

Twenty years later, a mother six times over, I opened my sewing box for a pair of scissors. In the rummaging, my hand brushed to cool surface of my grandmother's glass darning ball. Removing it, I held it on my palm. And I began to cry—not ordinary tears of nostalgia, but the awful rending sobs of mourning. No longer could I make a choice about sorrow or isolate the pain I'd lugged about for two decades. I had no power over the flood of agony that had pressed against the walls of my own building for so long. With effort, hours later, I dried my eyes and stilled the storm enough to prepare a meal and greet my family with my accustomed composure. I could not say to them, "I buried the only mother I ever knew this afternoon, and you will have to excuse me. I cannot cook." If my vulnerability had betrayed me, no need to share that frightening fact.

Marriage and motherhood are risky. You can get all tangled up in dangerous emotions without even knowing it's happening until it's too late. And striding along Route 1, I knew I'd been trapped once again, and that there was no exit from pain. But this was *natural*. It happened to everyone. Children grew up and became your friends instead of your tax deductions. It wasn't like death, sinister and selective. Maybe I could bear *this* pain. I would take it out and look at it. Lovingly I cupped each child in my mind. Some were hardy, born that way. Survivors by nature. Others were fragile. Too sensitive for this world. I trembled for them. One was a mixture, but the toughness always prevailed. Strange that I did not sort them by holiness, or intelligence, or personality—but by strength or lack of it. The ability to endure seemed so important to me. But I had knit these children about with prayer from the moment they'd become part of our home, whether by birth or adoption. I'd fasted and wept for their salvation. And, resting in the hand of God, who can sort the weak from the strong?

"They that wait upon the Lord shall renew their strength; they shall mount up with wings as eagles; they shall run, and not be weary; and they shall walk, and not faint" (Isa. 40:31).

They weren't all "waiting upon the Lord" at this point in their lives by any means, but I would "wait" for them, until the Holy Spirit did His gentle persistent work in their hearts.

Symbolically I let them go, blowing them like dandelion fluff from the palm of my hand, slowly, regretfully. I shed tears, and the wind blew them away, too.

I, also, must mount up with eagle's wings and let the past drop away. I must run and not be weary, and walk and not faint, but first I must wait upon the Lord. Start blossoming toward my God-center once again.

My thoughts were interrupted as I noted a fellow pedestrian coming toward me on the other side of the road. She was all woolen tweeds and proper walking shoes. Even a felt hat tilted jauntily.

As we came abreast she halted and smiled. "Hello. Do you have the time perhaps?"

I checked my watch. "Nine-twenty."

"Did you set out from Camden? I missed the ferry and decided to walk. It'a fair piece, isn't it?" How much farther do I have to go?"

"About an hour and a half, I'd say, depending on your pace. It's a great morning for the road, isn't it?" After I said it, I feared I sounded like one of the hoboes from my depression childhood.

"That it is. Where are you heading?"

"Belfast, hopefully. Are there motels along the way, in case I don't make it?"

"There are accommodations at Lincolnville Beach, but nothing much between there and Belfast I fear. 'Twill be quite a hike. Nice to have met you." Once more she set off at a brisk pace.

For a few moments I walked backwards, watching her stride along beneath the trees. I knew nothing of her except that she admired British fashions and that she was the kind of person who'd walk a few miles if she missed her ferry. That was almost enough. She'd never melt into a crowd, and I like people who don't melt into crowds. I wished she had asked me why I was hiking. Maybe in replying I'd have found the answer.

Watching her like this, I was risking embarrassment, but somehow I knew she'd not look back. She was all business, not a dreamer such as I. So I didn't turn till she rounded a bend. Momentarily, the road seemed a little lonely.

Now I noted water visible beyond the treetops, and cresting a low rise I found the ocean glittering to my right. Sun and sea and the sharp fall air blended into breathtaking rightness. Rocky and scrub-ridden, the land fell to the shore. In the distance I saw the cluster of buildings that was Lincolnville Beach. The deep, blue water looked wintry and cold. I loved the Atlantic. Love the way it roared over rocks and onto beaches as though it had stormed between continents on some mysterious urgent mission. This far north it never spit out any exotic shells, but it had a kind of grandeur beyond conchs and whelks. Wild and untamed, it asked for no man's admiration. It wasn't posing for Kodak. Nor did it curl shyly over the sand and tiptoe out again, back and forth, back and forth in warm, mesmerizing repetition, though I'd known summer days like that on beaches a bit farther south. Here it was fog and action and sound and a kind of harshness even in sunlight.

I was 9 when I first saw the sea. My grandparents decided on a rare holiday along with my great aunt and uncle. To leave home, the livestock, the routine of our days, was quite an event in itself. A Vermonter's life in 1937 contained no frivolity. The country was just getting to its knees from the depression, but I knew nothing of that then. We were poor, but I didn't know that, either. No bill collectors haunted our doorstep, and the cellar was always aglitter with my grandmother's canning jars. Her sewing machine provided our rather unglamorous wardrobes, and on occasion I had the high privilege of picking a dress from the Sears' catalog. So, what was "poor"? Using an outhouse perhaps and digging blocks of ice from sawdust for refrigeration. But those same blocks of ice provided homemade ice cream every summer Sunday. I guess the outhouse had no redeeming features, except that anyone who could brave the experience at thirty below was bound to become a person of fortitude.

At any rate, a three-day vacation was a definite luxury, and we prepared with all the anticipation one would muster for a European summer today. We crossed New Hampshire, viewing the Old Man of the Mountain as though it had escaped from Mount Rushmore. When we arrived at that point in Maine where the ocean smell began to tantalize the nostrils, I squeezed forward on my pinched perch between two middle-aged adults and knew something exciting was about to befall me. And the tang of salt air has affected me that way ever since.

After we found some cheap cabins that evening (motels were still only a spark in some entrepreneur's imagination) we sat on the porch and watched the gulls scrap and scream over the booty left behind by the tide. Trying to absorb it all, I didn't say much. Besides, in those days, kids weren't supposed to talk much, at least where I came from. My grandfather, freed momentarily from the pressures of life, lapsed into a joviality that left me open-mouthed. Who was this man who told funny stories on his sister that sent her into peals of laughter? They hardly knew I was there, those four adults, released from the rigid routines of their work-driven days. Each of them soaked up leisure thirstily, their parched selves hardly able to cope with the onslaught of unscheduled hours. For them it was a brief grab at a side of life that would never really be theirs. It was too late for them, but not for me. I loved Vermont's mountain ranges scalloping her skyline, rimming her valleys. They were knit into my being for all time, as every child's birthplace is. But there at York Beach, Maine, I came to understand there were a lot of things left to be seen, things perhaps as astonishing as this rocky, seaweed-strewn shore with its graceful gulls.

I longed to go right down to water's edge, but dusk was falling, and I was a bit in awe of this strange, new world. Besides, the adults would fuss and dole out somber cautions, so I contented myself with a visual orgy and later drifted off to sleep to a rhythmic crashing of the surf, which fell as naturally upon my ears as if I'd been born upon a beach.

It seemed only a few tumbles and turns later that I felt my grandmother shaking my shoulder in the semidarkness of dawn. "Wake up," she whispered. "We're going for a walk on the beach. If you hurry, we'll see the sunrise."

Sleepily I looked at the slumbering forms in the other beds. Obviously they weren't going anywhere. By "we," Gram meant herself and me. Like two conspirators, we would sneak away from conventional behavior and walk on that mysterious, beckoning sand at this ridiculous, black hour. In a flash I leaped from bed and fumbled for my clothing. We tiptoed out, stumbling over suitcases and shoes. Uncle Irving muttered, "What's going on?" as he turned over and put a pillow over his head.

Closing the door behind us, Gram and I burst into giggles. I couldn't believe she was doing this. "It's the ocean," she said as we stepped over the rocks separating the road from the beach. "It does something to me. Do you know what I'm talking about? Do you feel it?"

New Englanders didn't discuss elusive emotions they couldn't define, so it was strange conversation, but my answer came quick and unstudied.

"Yeah, I feel it."

And in a rare gesture of affection I took her hand, and we walked the beach like that, not talking, just watching the sky grow light, then peach and gold, and finally ablaze with a sun that rose up out of the sea like some mythical fiery beast. I learned the feel of wet hard sand and the icy chill of the Atlantic slapping over bare feet. And I saw shorebirds skittering in little bands, their tracks etching the sand in dainty designs, which the surf gobbled like *hors d'oeuvres* at its morning buffet.

Now, here, thirty-eight years later, the sea had drawn me from far inland to the rhythm of its shores. Oh, I had returned before with husband and children, but never alone. What would drive one to cut all ties with family and cast herself, a stranger, into the world? For the world really isn't geared to strangers. It's a civilization, even in our day of divorce and abortion, based on home and family. So why was I here? I had to answer the question before I could turn homeward. No, I had not rejected husband or child, or culture, or society, or God. Rather I was tired, fed up, confused, overwhelmed. Perhaps I'd come here to this spot on the Atlantic searching for that moment—that precise moment of childhood when I'd discovered the sea. For everything had been clear then. I had understood my relationship with the little handful of adults in my life. The future sprawled before me limitless and promising, possibilities glittering across it like daisies made of diamonds. Believing I experienced more, somehow, than they, I'd felt a kind of pity for the plodders. Sometimes I had felt so tuned in to the earth and everything going on about me that I wondered if I was made of a different clay than my fellow mortals. Color burned into me, and beauty was like food and drink.

And I would live forever.

Life eats deeply into such people. Eventually I learned there are others like me. People who live too intensely and burn out early. Every human contact extracts its due, because everything matters too much. So here I was fumbling backward in time, groping for a moment which had hovered bright as dawn's last star in the morning of my life.

Too much had happened and had all registered too sharply. Now sometimes I envied the plodders. I needed to sit on the shore and let it all drain away until I was a child again, empty and eager once more to be filled.

Lincolnville Beach was a tourist town in a third-rate movie. Some cabins perched on a hillside overlooking the sea (I had a momentary desire to rent one for a week and hike no farther, but ever I was aware of Amy counting the hours till my return. I could not shrug off motherhood, even temporarily. And I missed her, too, more than I cared to admit). A large nondescript restaurant, an Indian leather-and-bead shop, a post office, and a few other buildings huddled together. Bereft of vacationers, the village was as sleepy as any other New England town. It wasn't noon, but I was hungry, so I decided to eat on the cement slabs piled up as breakwater along the shore.

The contorted cheese sandwich I took from my pack drew the gulls, who demanded their share in raucous boldness, coming within inches of my hands. I admired their gray-white grace and pardoned their poor manners. Truthfully, I didn't care much for cheese sandwiches anyhow. Deciding to settle for an orange (a decision I would regret later on), I tossed hunks of sandwich to the beggars, who further displayed their lack of breeding by fighting over each piece.

Sheltered from the wind, my back against sunwarmed cement, I began to relax. the ocean glistened, slapping lazily against the breakwater. Having bolted their snack, the gulls dipped and hovered above me, hoping for some further offering. Peace drenched me. I should be on my way. Belfast was miles ahead. But I could not move. In this moment I was part of the earth, as much so as the bleached and broken shells wedged into cracks in the cement. Perhaps the debris of the years would ebb out to the sea with the tide. Sunlight penetrated deeply into my body, searching out the knots and coils, releasing them carefully, gently, until I was lulled into a warm euphoria. Even my mind dulled till ideas moved across it in slow motion, pausing for scrutiny upon request. What a strange, mixed-up creature I was, picking up pieces of the past and peering at them hopefully, as though they held answers. It was all so long ago. And even then life had been a mixture of sadness and delight. I could not ever remember a time when sadness stepped into the wings. She was always on stage, though during my child-raising years she'd had to settle for a supporting role, while delight took the lead.

Maybe we are *always* a little sad, because we are cut off from God. He made us to live forever, created us to bask in His love and thrive on His friendship. Then Eve's slim hand snapped the stem on a piece of fruit, and nothing has been right since. Not only must we grapple with death, but with guilt and an uneasy fear that we can never still, no matter how shrilly we laugh or how wildly we dance. We are sad because life, with its intensity of relationships and exquisite beauty, is a fleeting thing. So even while we are laughing, we are dying. To hold one's child and know that such overpowering love must someday be cut off is an agony we learn to ignore, for there is no other way. And to have known late afternoon sun glinting across still, deep waters, October's bright leaves dancing round, to then contemplate the finality of the grave is a sorrow too deep for confrontation, so we party longer and sing louder.

But worse than these sorrows is a *loneliness,* which we attempt to heal with all manner of devices, most of them designed simply to keep us from thinking. For more vital to us than relationship with parent, mate, or child is a relationship with God. We have been so long without it that we cannot define our unrest. Or verbalize it. Thus I never say to my friend, "I am so depressed today. I miss God." We do not know what it is to look into His eyes and see approval and affection and acceptance—we see Him only handing out to us the bloody skins of beasts to cover our nakedness. There is no debate about our unworthiness. Yesterday we lied. Today we lusted. Tomorrow we'll covet. It seems so obvious that we should avoid sin and reinstate ourselves in God's good graces until—as the years pass and the failures accumulate—we realize that sin is a disease inherent in our very beings, a matter over which we do not, after all, have much control.

The story is so sad that no author could have devised it—a helpless planet self-destructing slowly over centuries.

Only, as a Christian, I knew better. I knew another version of the story where God steps in. Where the bloody skins are only the first compassionate act in a long, unbelievable scenario of rescue. And I knew all about the Son, who stooped to become one of us, so realistically that He curled nine months in the dark warmth of a young woman's womb, just as any ordinary human. Can you believe that? One moment He was God, and the next a human fetus.

He walked the earth with common men, gently attacking their selfishness with His startling concepts of love. And He listened to women and took their problems seriously in an age when they didn't count. Little children clambered onto the lap of God and found Him kind.

But He didn't come just to *mingle* with us. The Son offered a cure for the sin disease at the cost of His life. He trembled at the risk—"If it be possible, let this cup pass from me"—but He never hesitated. This Being who tossed the planets and suns into the universe and thought humming birds into existence stretched His arms against the cross and let them pound nails into His calloused young carpenter hands. His royal-human blood dripped scarlet onto the rocks at His feet, and His muscled young body lifted and sagged against the pain while the Sabbath drew on and the rabble jeered.

Stepping away from all that was familiar and known, He swung out over the chasm, trusting in the slim cord of His Father's word. Falling, falling, falling—deep into the blackness of the second death, where no man had gone before, until the darkness consumed Him and stilled the taunts of men at last. Because that was the only cure. And He cared about us. Enough so that He couldn't be happy, even as the Prince of heaven, without us.

As a mother, if five of my six children are doing fine, but one is sick or unhappy or heading down a wrong road, I cannot fully enjoy the five until the sixth functions satisfactorily once more. I can feel his pain wherever I go. His sorrow or unrest sits like a stone upon my heart. I guess that's how it is with Him, too. In fact, the entire universe is still limping, because one tiny, lost planet continues to toy with its own rescue mission. Will it humble itself and be saved, or self-destruct? Suppose when rescue planes touched down on Iranian soil during that past crisis, the hostages had looked coolly at their deliverers and said, "We can look after ourselves, thank you. In fact, we rather like it here. Please don't interfere in our affairs."

That's sort of how we treat Christ. We appraise the cross with one of four reactions. Either (1) we simply reject the Bible account of our origins and our need of rescue, or (2) we decline to take any of it seriously, preferring to grab what we can from our brief life span and hope for the best when it's over, or (3) we *believe,* but somehow do not respond, putting off any meaningful contact with the Divine Liberator until death makes the decision for us. But those are only three responses. There *are* those who despise their captivity. Who recognize their inability to escape the doom of their fallen natures. (Such an aversion to sin is a gift the Holy Spirit urges upon everyone, but many of us are so frantically running hither and yon that we don't even hear His voice, much less receive His gift.) The cross to those individuals looms against the sky solid and enduring, inviting their scrutiny.

Suddenly I knew. Sitting there on the retaining wall with the Atlantic sloshing in from Europe, I knew everything depended upon our reaction to the cross. I must deal with my own response to the Crucified One. If there ever had been a day when I assumed I could order my spiritual growth, it was long past. Slowly, painfully, over the years I'd learned I was incapable of choosing whether or not to sin. I had experienced tremendous frustration. Determined to follow Christ, but unable. Cursing my weak self. Then, amazed at the malignancy of my disease, I'd scramble once more to my feet. I *would be* His person. Failure over and over again. Until at last I knew I was hopelessly, incurably ill. That all my vows and determinations were like 6-year-olds playing cowboys and Indians. They weren't *really* cowboys and Indians. Their guns were fake, their feathers were fake, and their clutching, rolling death scenes were fake. And so was my righteousness. The Bible called it "filthy rags."

A sea gull sat close to my foot, still, as though carved from wood. No longer begging. Just keeping me company. Or perhaps tolerating my presence in his world. At any rate, I liked him there. I wished all of life were as uncomplicated as this moment which he and I were sharing.

So here I was with my fake righteousness and a good clear knowledge of the cross. Why couldn't I put the two together? Wasn't that what Calvary was all about? Deliverance from sin? But somehow I never felt *really clean* even after I'd gone through the motions of confessional prayer. Probably because of all those failures. I knew I'd get up the next morning and do the same ugly things all over again. Something deep down inside me recognized a lack in this kind of experience.

If you've concluded by now that bank robbery was my vice, please understand that I'd left the *big*, obvious sins behind. The kind I was dealing with were quiet and inconspicuous and deadly. They sprang from selfishness and indifference. From greed and lack of compassion. And no human arsenal could rout them. My inability to cope with them had eroded my entire relationship with Jesus Christ. They were like the small lumps that remain in the bottom of my kitchen sifter after I have pulverized powdered sugar into a fine snowy heap. No amount of maneuvering of the bail over the wire mesh will reduce them to powder. Nothing but the firm steady thrust of my finger ever forces them through the screen. I needed the finger of God to force those stubborn sins out of my life, but God doesn't use force. He whispers and nudges and woos. And those methods weren't working, so the problem must lie with me. God evidently needed some kind of cooperation on my part. David's sure statement came to my mind. "Thy word have I hid in my heart, that I might not sin against thee." Was there a power in the Word of God to deliver from sin? I knew Peter's counsel to "desire the sincere milk of the word, that we may grow thereby" (1 Peter 2:2). But I wasn't the spiritual newborn he described. For thirty years I'd been a born-again Christian. *But perhaps—could it be?—I'd ceased to grow* after that first dazzling glimpse of my Lord. Perhaps I'd learned too briefly before I sought to teach. Could it be that I was locked into the sin situation because I had never opened myself, *as a needy recipient,* to the Word of God? Oh, I'd studied. The voice of the Spirit speaking through the rich King James prose had touched my heart again and again. And I had shared the insights with my children, in study groups, in books, in pulpits, wherever others would listen. *But to come to Holy Writ to be healed.* Perhaps I'd never done that. An excitement stirred within me. Naaman hadn't liked the idea of immersing himself in the muddy Jordan for healing. His own land had better streams. But in obeying, he'd found his cure. I too would go home and dip into the "Jordan" of Bible study to be healed. No, I would not neglect the simple, obvious measure, or rail at God for neglecting my growth.

"As the rain and snow come down from heaven, and do not return to it without watering the earth and making it bud and flourish, so that it yields seed for the sower and bread for the eater, so is my word that goes out from my mouth: It will not return to me empty, but will accomplish what I desire and achieve the purpose for which I sent it" (Isa. 55:10, 11, N.I.V.).

That was quite a promise. I would come for healing humbly, joyfully. It was nearly noon. I got to my feet. All the muscles of my body screamed to sit a bit longer, but I forced them into synchronization and started toward the highway.

A couple, perhaps in their early forties, walked

toward me, hand in hand, across the beach. They had ditched their shoes and socks, and their bare feet left imprints behind them in the moist sand. They were carefree and laughing. A moment of wrenching loneliness pierced me. I knew how Adam felt that day in Eden before Eve arrived. Surely God had planned man and woman to be together, dependent upon each other. Complementing each other. Ministering to each other's needs. In that original sinless Utopia those two innocents had had no need to fear mutual dependence, the specters of death and divorce not having yet invaded their sunlit world. But it was different now. Foolhardy to love unreservedly, what with humanity as frail and fickle as it is. Risk enters. The risk of pain and loss. Risk of rejection. So watch out, barefoot lady. This isn't Eden. There are no guarantees.

I headed toward the highway, which led out of town.

*   *   *   *   *

It was 6:25 P.M. when my feet hit the sidewalks of downtown Belfast. Weeks ago I had marked it on the map as my goal. Rockland to Belfast. But, expecting those miles to take me longer, to tire me more, I had underestimated my own stamina. Now I would have to decide whether to go on to Searsport or head home. At the moment, all I wanted was to shower and rest my weary body. I'd passed one neat motel on the outskirts of town but had rejected it in my eagerness to explore Belfast. Only now I would have no time for exploration. Dusk would soon be falling, and the idea of sleeping on the beach somehow didn't appeal to me. I needed food and lodging, and this was not Camden. No stately inn overlooked the harbor. When I checked at a local store that doubled as a bus depot for the earliest departing bus in the morning, the clerk assured me that I could purchase my ticket from the driver should I decide I had indeed come to journey's end.

84

Just be at the stop at 6:50 A.M.

That taken care of, I strolled along Main Street, wondering where I was going to find sleeping accommodations. I couldn't worry about food until that problem was solved. Something about the town made me uneasy. I'd seen it in my mind as an old sailing center—a quiet, quaint Maine seaport. But somehow it didn't have that feel at all. I guess I'd have said it seemed ominous, only that was ridiculous. This was New England, not Chicago. When I entered a small shop to make inquiry, I realized too late that I'd stumbled into one of those stores, heavy with incense, which pander to rock fans. But the long-haired young man at the counter was helpful, if a bit foggy. In between sips of his drink he informed me the closest motel was the one I'd passed on the way into town. There *were* others between Belfast and Searsport, in the other direction, but it would be a long hike. Would I like him to check The Breakers* to see if it still had an opening?

Yes, I'd be most grateful. Why, oh, why, hadn't I stopped on the way in? It must be a good mile or more back.

After fumbling through the phone book for a while, he picked up his drink and looked at me in total confusion. "What am I supposed to be looking for?"

"The Breakers?" I offered hopefully. "A reservation for me?"

"Of course." Courtesy, even kindness, filled his voice. He found the number, and after dialing clumsily, carried on a brief conversation with the motel's manager.

"She's still got a room, but she won't hold it. It's first come, first served." He eyed my pack with troubled eyes.

---

* Not the real name of the motel.

A LITTLE JOURNEY

"You walking?"

"Yeah."

"Then you'd better hurry. This town doesn't offer much for tourists, and it's no place to spend the night on a park bench." I could feel his concern.

"Don't worry. I'll head right out there. You've been so kind. Thank you."

Nodding, he went back to his drink. Ten minutes later he would not remember the sunburned woman with a bright orange backpack, but I would not forget his confused gentleness for a long time. Back on the street everyone seemed, by comparison, hurried and harsh.

Moving hastily along the sidewalk, I realized, somewhere in the residential section, that two youngsters were tagging along behind.

"Hi," I greeted, turning to walk backward for a moment. "Why don't you come alongside and talk to me?"

Shyly, two small girls matched their pace with mine.

"Where'd you come from, lady?"

"Well, I've been walking along Route 1 from Rockland, but my real home is not far from Niagara Falls." I tried to pick a landmark they'd recognize.

"Really?" They looked at me as if I'd fallen from outer space. "Why are you walking?"

There, at last someone had asked the question.

"Because I've always wanted to hike some place I've never been before." I hesitated. "And I'm not getting any younger, so it was now or never. And besides I had some things to think about."

"Oh," the smaller girl said, satisfied.

"Where are you going to sleep tonight?" the elder asked.

"At The Breakers if I get there while there's still

room." I quickened my pace.

"That's a long way." The younger girl looked up at me through squinted dark eyes.

"It isn't either." The older child cast her sibling a scornful glance. "It's just a couple blocks and then on by a little stretch of field," she said to me, one adult to another. "We'd better go back. Ma'll be mad if we walk too far."

Now I missed their small bodies skipping along beside me, and their innocent curiosity. Maybe it wasn't such a bad town after all.

The motel sat back from the road quite a distance. Enjoying the last late rays of afternoon sunlight, I walked the long entrance, relieved that shelter would soon be mine.

As I stepped into the office a woman entered from a side room. A small, neat woman with worry etched deeply into every feature.

"I'm looking for a room for the night," I said.

"You hiking?" she asked, eyeing my pack.

"Yes."

"Alone."

Something was making her nervous, and not knowing what it was disturbed me.

"Yes, I'm alone," I admitted, wondering what difference it made. She dropped her head and a long moment of silence followed. Finally obviously having struggled with a decision, she looked up and almost smiled. "I have a place for you. Let me get the key."

Moments later we entered a not-unpleasant room, heavy with the stale odor of cigarettes. I noted it backed up to the office. She placed clean towels in a tidy pile on one bed. Again I sensed a hesitancy on her part. I knew she was trying to say something—or not to say something. At last she spoke.

"My apartment is right out behind. You can see it

from your back window." Vaguely she pointed beyond the drapes, and then paused, sorting words once more. "If you should need me in the night, just holler." As she slipped out the door she left me with some uneasy questions. Why in the world would I need her in the night? Had she been watching too many horror movies on TV? I would have bet my best hiking sneakers she lived under some kind of strain. Never had I seen it written more clearly on a person's face.

Low sunlight streamed between the slats of the venetian blinds onto blue floral bedspreads. I cranked windows open to let good sea air duel the pollution within. Hunger consumed me. Hours, miles, and one lonely orange stood between me and that early breakfast in Camden. There was no restaurant in the area, so I could do nothing but dig into my bag for the last small packs of trail mix. My friend, Phyllis, who runs a health-food store back home in New York State, had lovingly packed them for me, and it was her top grade, rich with dried apricots and plump pecans among the lesser nuts and fruits. It had looked inviting indeed as I'd tucked it among the necessities of my pack in preparation for my trip. Now I wondered how I was going to survive on it. I wanted mashed potatoes and homemade bread. Something to stick to my ribs. In fact, I'd settle for a bowl of shredded wheat and bananas. Anything but sunflower seeds and raisins. Thinking perhaps by then I'd be famished enough to be grateful, I decided to take a shower.

When I came out of the steamy bathroom a half hour later, dusk had arrived and with it the gloom that befell me each night. Morosely munching pecans and knowing I'd soon be down to soy nuts, I walked to the front window. Nearly every parking space at the motel was full. That seemed odd for an off-season September night. Vans and pickups outnumbered cars. And the licenses were all State of Maine. What kind of motel was this? Refusing to let my imagination get out of control I decided to watch television pretending I'd had a good meal and all the little crunchies were just a TV snack.

But I never had liked the Waltons, and now they only added to my restlessness. I would call home. Desperately I wanted to hear familiar voices. I was ready to go home. Not just because it was night, but because I'd come to that spot on the map that had been my destination. At least in terms of miles, I had completed what I'd set out to do.

All my airline tickets were for Sunday, and tomorrow was only Friday. Was that a problem? Just one of the many things I didn't know about travel. Well, I'd find out soon enough.

Noisy groups of men in work clothes passed my window steadily, the office door clattering behind them as they entered. If there were any other women in the place besides jittery Jane and myself, I'd failed to see them. Although I dreaded returning to the office, that's where the phone was, and I was determined to use it.

The moment I entered the room, I knew I did not belong there. Silence settled over the men, who were drinking and playing cards. As I walked toward the phone at one end of a long counter I felt their stares. The dialing rattled into utter stillness. I thought surely, out of courtesy, they'd resume their boisterous conversation once more, but a kind of curious hostility hung in the air, and not a sound disturbed it.

On the other end I heard my husband accepting the collect call, his familiar voice in its safe, comfortable setting. I could even hear the supper dishes rattling in the background, interspersed with youthful banter. *Home* on the end of a telephone cord, just waiting to be reeled in.

"Hi," he said, pleasure tinging his control. "Where are you?"

"I'm in Belfast. I made it. It wasn't as far as I had expected."

"Do you have a place for the night?"

"I'm staying at a motel called The Breakers on the edge of town."

"Are you okay?" I knew he meant Did I have blisters—was I crawling on all fours? Not Was I OK in a strange motel filled with ruffians?

"I'm fine—a little sunburned, a little hungry, but fine." I couldn't dump it on him. This was *my* problem, not his. Neither did I wish to admit my fears to my eavesdropping audience.

"Guess what?" I lowered my voice. "I'm coming home tomorrow if I can catch the right flights. Could you take time off to meet me at the airport?"

It took him by suprise. He couldn't hide his delight. "You bet I can. What airport? When?"

"I don't know. But I'll call you before I leave Boston if everything works out."

"Are you sure you're ready to come home?" He had to know it was resolved, whatever had driven me away.

"I'm ready," I said, knowing part of me would always walk the highway searching, while another part ran home to welcoming arms.

"I've missed you." Love and concern filled his voice, and I knew I'd asked a lot of my family. I'd not prepared them for this kind of unconventional behavior. They didn't know the person who had needed so desperately to know herself. And they'd never, perhaps, feel so safe with her again.

"I've missed you, too. It's been a strange week. I'll tell you all about it later. Give my love to the kids."

I hated to place the receiver on the hook, to let go of security and walk the gauntlet of those eyes.

90

* * * * *

Back in my room, I opened my Bible. If there was healing for sin, I wanted to find it. I had to go home with some answers. Something I could get my teeth into. I was weary of nebulous nothings. Immediately I turned to Romans. Often in Paul's scholarly oratory I'd caught glimmers of something hopeful, something I'd hardly dared believe. Over and over I'd read chapter 9, verses 30-33, and chapter 10, verses 1-3. Somehow Israel had failed to please God because of her insistence upon working out her own righteousness. I had an uneasy feeling I, too, had operated in that fashion all my life. Then I thought of Israel's first arrival upon the borders of Canaan and the people's cowardly fear of the inhabitants. Their pitiful turning back into the wilderness because the giants looked bigger to them than the God who had piled up the Red Sea and hovered over their camp in a fiery cloud. Unbelief brought them another forty years of stumbling around in the sand and the death of almost everyone over 20. It cost them *everything*. All they had dreamed of and struggled toward for so long. Doubt did them in. And generations later it did it again when Messiah made His appearance a little differently than they'd anticipated.

Doubt was the enemy.

It could do *me* in too.

I could lose everything.

Did Paul's emphasis on Israel's failure really have any application in my life? Was it related to my inability to overcome sin? And was it possible I too had attempted to carve out for myself a spotless character through sheer willpower? It was scary to leave the "giants" up to God. I wasn't sure I could do that. What if He never dealt with them or didn't realized how deeply embedded they were?

So—unbelief was *my* problem, too. I'd had to walk

some weary miles and end up in a crumby motel to isolate it.

The noise level in the next room had risen appreciably. Drunken laughter and yelling intermingled. I feared it would be a long night.

Perhaps here in this alien room, cut off from the secure and familiar, I could accept Jesus Christ as my Saviour. Thirty years before, I had *given myself to Him.* But I realized now that that was only half of the total Christian experience. At the same time I should have *taken Him,* His righteousness, His power to re-create, as *His* contribution to the relationship . . . His gift to me.

With the racket next door growing more out of control by the moment, I struggled to find Messiah, the One who would give me a new heart. As though through a keyhole, I saw something wondrous. A new kind of life where I could rest. (What was it Hebrews 3 said? That Israel could not enter His *rest* because of their unbelief? See also Hebrews 4:3-11.) *That's* what the cross was all about! Giving up the struggle and accepting the gift. Entering into a *rest*—I hardly dared to think of such a release, much less reach out and take it. I had been raised on sterner stuff. Fine old New England saws like "God helps those who help themselves" and "If you want a thing well done, do it yourself." Excellent counsel for secular life, but, for the first time, I realized it had hovered like a gray fog over my entire Christian experience. I had tried. Oh, *how* I had tried to be a proper follower of Jesus Christ. While I suspected I'd even fooled a lot of people, I'd never fooled myself or God. Born a sinner, I could no more cure myself of that than I could of cancer. In fact there is more hope for the cancer victim than there is for the sinner to save himself.

A terrible crash in the next room startled me, heart hammering, into an upright position on the bed. Along with the noise of an upturned chair or table came the thud of a body hitting the wall and then the floor. Fierce profanity invaded my meditation. Voices, razor-sharp with anger, sliced through flimsy walls till I felt myself almost a part of the devilish din on the other side. What a strange place to accept the saving blood of Jesus! (I wished I were brave enough to go next door and offer it to the brawling men.)

Once more I lay down, strangely at peace. My watch said 1:30 A.M.

"Thank You, Lord, for taking care of me in this unlikely place. Help me to allow You to re-create me. Surely I will meddle in your work. I am that kind of person. I often do jobs that I might easily assign to others because I am never quite sure they will be done to suit me. How arrogant that is, Lord. How supremely haughty I've been to question Your creative powers in my behalf. Forgive me. Can I really rest? You will do it all?

The magnitude of such a possibility boggled my mind. A healing and renewing going on within me all apart from my own efforts? A miracle indeed! That was what I needed. A miracle. So what was *I* supposed to do while it was happening. Just go home and wash windows and cook lasagna and do my monthly column and hope to grind out a book now and then? Surely I could help with the reconstruction in some innocuous way. Even the best Carpenter can use someone to hand Him nails?

I tried to think of the wickedest woman Jesus ever dealt with here on earth. The woman at the well? The one taken in adultery? They'd both lost the respect of their fellow humans. Yet Jesus did not reject them. He forgave, delivered, and somehow so met their deepest needs that they no longer sinned. It occured to me those two had something in common besides their promiscuous lifestyles. When they met Jesus, they had *time* for Him. Time to listen. The Samaritan gal could have poured Him His water and hustled back to her shady relationship, but she didn't. She stayed with her unusual new Acquaintance until the realization that He was the Messiah burst upon her thirsty mind.

And Mary, that black sheep from the respectable Bethany family—what shame she had endured. Yet He had found compassion for her too. Obviously sinners did not repulse this man-shaped God. He offered *rest*. Time to recoup: Time to think without the burden of accusation. Time to turn homeward, limping, bruised, but experiencing the first sweet whisperings of hope, And in such an atmosphere of forgiveness they were ready to listen. Gratitude flung them at His feet. Mary *listened* while Martha cooked. Why should Martha listen? She was "good" already. Or was she? But Mary, fresh from the pits of sin, knew her place of safety. Right at the feet of Jesus absorbing His kingdom.

So maybe that's what "handing the nails" was all about. Just staying with Him. Opening one's self to His promised cleansing. But for me there'd be no sitting by the well, or under the grape arbor. No hearing the loved sound of His voice. No watching an occasional smile light the serious lines of His young face. I'd have to find Him as David had, through His written word. Through prayer. Through the witness of Christian friends. Through preaching. Through sharing. "Handing the nails" would not be easy. I knew from hard experience that the enemy has a thousand distractions. Over and over again I'd find myself in the kitchen with Martha.

I'm not sure I can even sit at Your feet, Lord. This world is like a great vacuum sucking me into busyness. Nice safe, legitimate activities that keep my mind off You. The miracle must go very deep, Lord. You must understand the extent of my helplessness. I *choose* Your rest. I *accept* Your death in my behalf. Your righteous life in place of mine. That is all I can do. I cannot promise I can even be a Mary in my devotion. I may get all tangled up in the menu department—or in the do-gooder department—or even the time-frittering department. What if I go home and nothing changes? I'm scared that's how it will be. Scared I'll lose the wonder of tonight and my emancipation. I *want* to put You first. I *want* to be a living example of what You can do with a hopeless human. I would like that to be my gift of gratitude for deliverance from fear and guilt and loneliness. But I'm not even sure I can give that gift. I'm not sure of anything, Lord, except that You are my only hope. Can you take me like that? No promises. There's an old hymn my grandmother used to sing: "Nothing in my hand I bring, Simply to Thy cross I cling." That's right where I am, Lord. I come to You that poor.

The noise next door began to spew out of the office and down the sidewalk alongside my window. Raucous laughter and coarse voices assaulted the peaceful night as the men scuffled toward their rooms. Evidently, at 2:40 A.M., they had decided to call it a day.

At last stillness released the small night sounds, but I could not lie awake to listen. I must be up by six o'clock if I was to catch the bus that would bear me home. With no alarm on which to depend, I slept fitfully, arousing every now and then to check the time.

THE SIXTH DAY

6 It seemed only a toss and a tumble until dawn nudged me from sleep and into my travel-weary clothes. The abbreviated night had taken its toll. I was light-headed from lack of sleep and nourishment, and my legs definitely weren't cooperating fully. That is, until I hit the out of doors. The cool, fresh sea air was a tonic potent as any herbal brew. Fog hung filmy and mysterious over the harbor town. Heading down the long driveway, I looked back, just once, at the trucks and vans lined up before the now peaceful motel. Last night's bizarre events seemed a dream—yet the license plates all said State of Maine.

Walking briskly along beside the fine old homes rising eerily out of the fog, I'd never felt better. The vagabond within campaigned for the open road. "You could head inland," she whispered, "and explore some country lanes or continue on up the coast. Think of all those waiting bends in the road, the little villages, and the new people. You'll never have this chance again." And she was right. I never would. The elixir of anticipation mingled with physical vigor would not likely come my way again. But I would go home. Back to responsibility and those I loved. I wasn't sure why. Another few days wouldn't have mattered. It wasn't loneliness, or even last night's Hitchcockian overtones, that were turning me homeward. I'd come to terms with the loneliness, recognizing it as a temporary, after-dusk affliction. And I'd known right from the start I would face some slight element of danger as a woman traveling about on foot. No, those factors weren't part of my decision. Somewhere at gut level I knew the troubled questions that had driven me here in the first place had been resolved, not in specifics, but in broad generalities from which I could refine conclusions and fabricate a pattern for the final third of my life. With that knowledge I could afford to ignore the rebel within whose feet itched for the sandy shoulders of Route 1.

Belfast looked and smelled at this early hour as I had imagined it would. It had the tangy aroma of a sea town, and the lifting mists revealed an aura of age and stability about its architecture, at least in this residential sector. As I neared the center of town, workmen hailed each other in profane friendly greeting and the smell of coffee drifted faintly on the air. Though it's not my beverage, it awakened sleeping taste buds and reminded me my diet had been a bit deprived of late. But I would not have time to eat before boarding the bus, so I decided not to think about food.

As I neared the bus stop the form of a young woman appeared out of the fog. She was nicely dressed and carried a small suitcase, so I assumed she, too, was awaiting the promised Greyhound. Upon close appraisal, I decided she couldn't be more than 18 or 19.

"Is the bus usually on time?" I asked, to break the silence.

"Yes, ma'am." Her deference made me feel old. "It starts out here in Belfast, so it's seldom late."

It seemed awkward, just the two of us there in the fog, so I nursed a conversation. "Are you traveling far?"

She came to life at the simple question, her pretty face growing absolutely radiant as she answered. "My boyfriend goes to college in Boston, and I'm going to visit him for the weekend." Her happiness lit the gray morning like Fourth of July sparklers.

"Do you live here in town?"

"Just a few blocks from here," she said, indicating the direction with a wave of her hand. "But my mom drove me down this morning. She won't let me walk anywhere. This is a rough town."

"Really? I've always thought of Belfast as a sleepy little seaport."

She gave me a look I recognized as one teenagers reserve for pitifully naive adults. "This year we've had a murder, a rape, and several muggings right on these streets. You just don't go out walking at night."

"That's sad. If you can't stroll about of an evening in a little New England town, what's gone wrong with the world?"

"It used to be like you thought, just a nice friendly little town. When I was small, we often played out after dark on summer nights, but a lot of strange people have moved into the area. Everything's changed." For the first time she took a good look at me. "Where did you come from? Are you hiking?"

"Well, I wandered up from Rockland over the past few days. My home is near Buffalo, New York. I just needed to get away and sort out some things in my mind for a bit. Now I'm heading home."

"Where'd you stay last night?"

"At a place called The Breakers on the edge of town."

Her eyes widened. "You didn't! That place is no real motel. It's just a hangout for some of the roughest characters around town. They *live* there. I wouldn't spend a night there for any amount of money. Couldn't you tell it was no place for a woman?"

"Along about midnight I began to catch on," I said, grinning. "It was noisy, but no one bothered me."

"And then you walked alone all the way back into

town at this hour in the fog?" Her tone was parental and scolding. I was beginning to feel like a juvenile delinquent.

"Well, it seemed harmless enough to me at the time. I had no idea of your crime rate here." I was making a little joke, but she didn't find it funny.

"I'm not fooling, ma'am. You just don't walk around this town alone unless the sun's high in the sky." I knew it was quite possible this youthful citizen of Belfast was putting me on, but on the other hand, it *had been* quite a night.

"Well, at any rate, I survived, and here comes the bus." We clambered on and she sat far in the back. I chose the very front seat, where I had a panoramic view of the coastline and its waking towns. The girl and I had no further contact. She probably told her boyfriend about an irresponsible woman she'd met who was living back in another century and was lucky to be alive. Somehow it didn't all seem quite that dramatic to me.

The journey rewound far too quickly. As the familiar sights, engraved upon my vision as I'd walked, now sped by in reverse, I realized how important this trip had been to me. Painful, joyous, enlightening, and healing. I'd been lonely, sometimes frightened. But at home I had had moments of frustration and longings for I knew not what. Perhaps we are never really at peace here in the world since Eve took the fruit in Eden. The fear that sent her hiding from God afflicts us all. We are trespassers on an estate created to be our home. And even though no one orders us out, we are still trespassers. It breeds in us an uneasiness, an inability to enjoy completely even the best moments of our lives.

Christ came to change that. To ensure us adoption back into the royal family. And with the adoption comes a measure of peace. We are no longer trespassers on the estate, but something terrible still has happened—that has not yet changed. Where once all was joy and song, beauty and loving relationships, we now find murder, sorrow, weeds, hate, illness, and death. Our adoption does not change that fact, though it does transform our attitude toward it. God strengthens us to live among the shadows, but always it's easier with a companion—a parent, a mate, a child, a friend. And thus dependence becomes a part of life, with all its accompanying potential for pain and loss. I'd experienced that pain too early and too often. Now I feared it more than I feared loneliness. So I'd left everyone I'd valued most behind, to see if I were still intact without them. Unfortunately, I hadn't done very well. Had I been cut off permanently from home ties I'd have been a basket case. *I was vulnerable.*

Years before, when our marriage was young, my husband had been drafted into the Army during the Korean war. Because I had a good job, we decided it would be practical for me to stay at home and work while he did his two-year stint for Uncle Sam. Though my own family—what little there was of it—was hundreds of miles away, Don's family lived close by and gave me total caring support. I liked my work and my coworkers and lived upstairs over an elderly couple who treated me like a daughter. Nevertheless, I began to develop some rather vague physical symptoms. I, who had in childhood drawn safely back from the human race, knew not the definition of mourning. Taking what was good in life, I had sidestepped anything that could possibly hurt. Therefore, my unbearable pain at the loss of my husband had to find its release in physical ways because I refused to deal with it. Every door to normal grieving had long closed. The weakness, headaches, and loss of appetite finally drove me to a doctor who ordered up an array of tests and bloodletting, all to no avail. Frustrated, I went to another physician. Older and wiser than the first, he appraised my records thoughtfully for a bit, then asked me curtly, "Have you tended to be sickly throughout your life?"

"No."

"Have you experienced some traumatic event in the past year?"

I thought about that one a bit. "Well, my husband went into the service a few weeks ago, but that's hardly what you're after, I'm sure."

He lifted his head and looked me right in the eye. "Young lady, you are missing your husband whether you know it or not. Can you go where he is?"

Thoughts of our burgeoning bank account and our tidy plans flashed through my mind. "As soon as he finishes basic training I could go."

"Then go." He shuffled my papers into a folder, and I knew his mind was already on the next patient.

As I walked from his office into the sunlight a terrible weight fell from my shoulders, and I had all I could do not to dance down the sidewalk. I was going to be with Don. Nothing could stop me. Not even our sensible plans. Hadn't the doctor *ordered* me to? No one could argue with that. And I went. And I never had the headaches and nausea again. But I learned something frightening. I discovered that loss can not only cause the emotional pain I'd experienced in childhood, but it can also make one ill. It is extremely dangerous to love. That lesson seemed to receive reinforcement around every bend.

Now, many years later, I had not forgotten. But another truth dawned upon me. The greatest happinesses of my life sprang from those moments when love forced itself beyond the barriers in my heart. Moments when I'd abandoned caution and loved freely and fiercely, whether mate, friend, or child, such as the times when I'd settled into a living room chair to watch the 11:00 P.M. news with our teenagers. After the TV had ground out its grim fare, we'd talk a bit before going to bed. There'd be jokes and laughter, and a serious comment or two on the news. Sitting there, with the lamplight softening faces, I'd think how strong the ties of family. Each of us moving out into new areas of living, yet knit together irrevocably by all that we'd shared. Eventually we'd all be separated, each wrestling with life in his own way, but the high moments and the ordinary days we'd lived together would be part of us forever. I loved our children in those moments in a spendthrift way, all guards down.

Sometimes, picking raspberries with my husband or walking with him through the orchard, the same sense of completeness catches me for an instant. And I know that all true joy, all security, this earth can offer lies in family or close friendships. The cost is high—the risk of eventual pain and separation. One cannot love without taking that risk.

Riding this bus homeward, Lord,
I lay down my independence.
I need not only You;
I need members of the human community also.
Help me to accept being cared for,
for the truth is I'm not strong,
capable, confident, or wise.
Only needy.
Why is it so hard to be needy?
My liberated friends will not like this
conclusion.
Not even most of my Christian friends.
They think dependence
makes you a zero person.
But You were dependent
when You were part of our human family.

You said You could do nothing without
Your Father.
You spend whole nights in prayer.
You were needy, too.
You needed John's love
and the little home in Bethany
where You could relax among friends.
You needed the Dove
and the Father's assurance
that You were the Beloved Son.
But Your need didn't render You incapable.
The strength You drew upon Your knees
changed lives,
healed the sick,
and set men free.
Maybe that's the secret.
When at last we fall down
and give up
and say
    I need,
    I fear,
    I fail.
Maybe then, and only then,
You can pick us up
and dust us off
and dry our tears
and begin to let Your power
flow into us
and through us
to the world.

As the bus made its way through the outskirts of
Portland I experienced a bit of uneasiness. My plane
reservations were all for the following Sunday. How
was I going to find flights that would have me home by
nightfall? Not only would I have to experience a stroke

of luck here in Portland, but Boston airport would have to also treat me well.

In a cab, hurtling between the station and airport, the driver, having noted my pack and sunburned nose, plied me with questions. "Where have you been?"

"Walking up the coast toward Belfast.",

"Alone?"

"Alone."

"I beg your pardon, ma'am, but you must be crazy."

"I've already heard that once before today in a little gentler version. A girl at the bus stop in Belfast told me it was a rough town."

"The entire Maine coast is a rough town. A lot of hippie types have drifted into this area. No one bothers them here. It's been a bummer for the whole area."

"I grew up in Vermont." I flinched as, changing lanes in fast-moving traffic, he squeezed between two large trucks. "It's hard for me to visualize New England as anything but a quiet, conservative corner of the country. I somehow can't fit hippies or violence into the picture. I guess I'd have to get mugged to believe it, though I did spend a rather eerie night in Belfast."

He looked in the mirror at me. "I owned a small flower shop here in Portland for a long time. About three years ago it began to be vandalized. It happened so many times that I eventually faced financial disaster, so I sold out while there was anything left to salvage. I've been driving a cab ever since. So, lady, if you saw it all like it used to be, count yourself blessed. And it's true the pines and the gulls and the surf haven't changed. And the nice old Colonial homes. It's just the people who've changed. Not the natives." The cab driver chuckled. "We're the same old bullheaded, hardworking Republicans we've always been. Even the tourists are OK. They come up and gawk at the scenery and give our economy a shot in the arm. And they mind their business. It's these drifters that are doing us in. They don't respect nothin' or contribute nothin'. They just *take,* any way they can get."

I hoped he didn't think I was one of the drifters. Tipping him generously as he dropped me at the airport, I wished him well. He was typical of the hardy lot with which I had been raised. No crying over what couldn't be helped. An acceptance of life just as it came, the good and the bad. It wasn't religion. Just a lifestyle practiced for centuries by a stoic people in a harsh land.

The airport was small but busy. Taking my Delta ticket to the proper counter, I inquired hopefully for a flight to Boston. The agent shook his head, not even bothering to look up. No empty seats on any Boston flight that afternoon.

What *was* I doing here? I who knew nothing of the intracacies of travel even under the best of circumstances? What ever made me think I could plane hop home without reservations?

Noting a line at the next counter, I decided to join it. I had, it seemed, all day. No destination. No schedule. Maybe I'd go to Tampa or Phoenix. Not really. I wanted to go home.

"Where is this flight headed?" I said to the mother of two ahead of me.

"Boston," she replied, darting me a quick puzzled glance as she hoisted her toddler a bit higher on one hip.

"I've had a little change in plans," I explained, none too coherently, "and I'm trying to get to Rochester, New York, via Boston. Maybe I'll get lucky." When I smiled at the baby, he burrowed his head shyly into his mother's neck.

By the time I arrived at the counter the flight was boarding.

"Yes, I have a seat, and yes, I will accept a ticket from another airline," the uniformed young man assured me, "but the plane's about to leave, and you'll never get your luggage checked through in time."

"I don't have any luggage." I pointed to the pack on my back. "I'm traveling light."

He made hasty notations on my ticket and cautioned me to move quickly. When I squeezed in beside a businessman on the crowded plane I was a little drunk on good fortune. The first hurdle was past and I had managed by myself. I'd not succumbed to fear or pessimism as was my tendency. Only as an adult had it been my tendency, however. As a teenager I'd been confident. Why had I lost that?

My seatmate was deep in Gail Sheehy's *Passages*.

"How's the book?" I asked. "According to the reviews I remember, it's a winner." Although I didn't really want to chat, it always seems awkward sitting elbow-to-elbow with someone for long stretches without any communication.

"Excellent." Obviously he was telling the truth, for he barely lifted his eyes from the page. I took my cue and was well content with the arrangement.

As the plane sped down the runway and thundered into the sky, I realized I'd taken no medication for airsickness, yet still felt fine. No forced yawning, no chewing gum, no nasal spray for inner-ear problems. Instead I was enjoying the powerful lift, the slight sideward tilt, the miraculous leap from earth to sky that is twentieth-century flight. I had always known that airsickness, for me at least, was in part related to apprehension. Why was I no longer afraid? Back in New York, safely ensconced in my husband's thoughtful care, I would become a coward again. I loved his protectiveness, didn't want to ever live without it, but I hated the bondage of timidity it birthed in me. The problem was mine, not his. Somehow I must learn to be cared for, yet retain my inherent confidence at the same time. Something to pray about.

"For God did not give us a spirit of timidity, but a spirit of power, of love and of self-discipline" (2 Tim. 1:7, N.I.V.).

Below, along the coast, I observed the long, slow build of pressure and power slamming waves into airy fountains over massive rocks. My life at home had felt that way, as though I were being hurled against the rocks and broken into fine spray. It hadn't happened overnight. Nothing was drastically different in my life, except that some of our older children had come home to live after being away at school for several years. Suddenly I just hadn't been able to cope anymore. Like the sea swells below, the pressure had been growing slowly. The unceasing hard work, the emotional strains of a large, multiracial family, my own personal struggles to be God's person and to meet everyone's needs. That was my nature—to *be there* for everyone. A highly idealistic and impossible goal, as Don had pointed out to me patiently and painstakingly many times. My mind understood, but I kept on trying.

The very nature that made me a writer also made me too sensitive to the growing pains of my children. I'd shed too many tears in the long, quiet nights. (One son had chided me repeatedly throughout his uproarious teens, "Why do you take it all so *personally?"*) I hadn't learned how to move in on the swells and be broken over the rocks. The waves shatter and fall back, frothing, into the sea. Someday, somewhere, they will hurl once more against some other shore, but in between they rest. I had run from the hurling.

Now, temporarily away from the rocks, able to look at the overall coastline of my life, I realized I had nearly reached that place of falling back and moving toward another shore.

Life has many turning points. We must make the

awkward step from childhood to adolescence, then another from our teens into independence. How painfully, sometimes cruelly, we fight against our fears of leaving home and parental care. A psychologist friend once told me that the more we love our parents, the more brutal the struggle to be free. So that's a crucial turning point.

Marriage is another. The melting and molding of lifestyles. Dying a bit, to live more fully.

Children force us to turn again. To die a little more for a new kind of love. A richer, laughing, singing, more fulfilling love than we ever dreamed of. It's a gift and a wonder and a miracle. But it has a price. It hurls you against the rocks again and again. Especially so as they move toward adulthood, rejecting, at times, parental values and lifestyles.

Then suddenly life ebbs. The house quiets. We make our peace with our careers, our child-raising, maybe even with our spiritual selves. I had not arrived at that ebbing, but I was getting close. The relentless pounding had left me weary. But I knew in my heart of hearts that this final turning would be the greatest test of all. The loneliness of a vacated house, the challenges of a marriage long used to the roller-coaster rhythms of child-raising, the assault of old age, the facing of death. Death, with his final question. "What *do* you believe, and how does it relate to this gasping, painful moment of farewell?"

I had made the other turnings with a fair amount of grace, though total honesty forces me to admit that Don and I, as two only children, didn't settle immediately into a rose-covered cottage with the cooings of turtle doves. Sometimes we lashed out angrily, and sometimes we bludgeoned each other with silence. But other times we went to the library, picked out a colorful variety of books, bought a pint of ice cream apiece on the way home, and sat propped up in bed reading and digging into the buttercrunch through sweet, companionable hours. We had little money, but we were rich in love, and we were learning how to live with that love and all its healthy demands. And we're still learning.

I turned naturally, so very naturally, into child-raising, though the sleepless nights sometimes temporarily blurred my maternal instincts. But I loved the blossoming of awareness, the innocence, the trusting, loving ways, of little ones. Later I reveled in their emerging personalities, their wit, their interest in the world beyond their rural home. Consequently I do not understand young couples today who say they want no children. I try to tell them that life without a child is no life at all.

My real problem was not the mild rebellion against household servitude that originally had prompted my trip, but rather my need to come to terms with the woman I had become and with the remainder of my life. What had I done with my forty-eight years? What would I do with the remaining thirty (if I was lucky)? Had these few strange, lonely, gypsy, carefree, happy days provided any answers, any insights?

The girl was gone forever. I had not found even the ghost of her in the soft coastal fogs, that sad, sensitive, independent, funny, irreverent young woman who'd strutted into life with much bravado and a terrible ache in her heart.

Marriage had healed, to a great extent, the scars of a bittersweet childhood. God provided a man who saw me as bright, pretty, and interesting, and however great a miracle that demanded on God's part, it was just what I needed. Don, his background as secure as mine had been erratic, knew a stability I had never experienced. Down through the years he'd calmly put the pieces back together when the pressures of life left me shattered.

A LITTLE JOURNEY

Once in our early marriage, lying in the darkness of one small apartment or another, we talked of our childhoods. Of the park in which he'd learned to play football, and the country road I'd walked to and from school. We explored all the years before we'd met, shared the people who'd touched our lives, and marveled that we'd found each other. Somehow we came to parents, and spoke of *his* father, who'd died soon after our marriage. Then *my* father, who was alive, but dead to me. I tried to tell him how it had come about, this death of a relationship, but I could not, because I did not know. It was one of the mysteries in life, like the Incarnation and the miracle in a seed. Whatever had happened took place before I reached an age of awareness—which was not fair. I kept working to reach him during my little-girl years, trying to be smart (all those glistening report cards) and good. Never to make waves. As I told Don all this in the stillness of night, a dam broke in my heart and I wept and ranted, totally out of control, tearing the past to shreds with the pent-up agony of twenty years.

I never knew who I was, so I could never find my place in the family. Though I lived beneath their roof and they could not have been kinder, I was not my grandparents' child. I was *his* child, but he denied it with his indifference, his cool rejection year after year. That rejection was a gaping hole in my life for which there was no mending, not even a patch. Everyone else in the clan had a slot. But I stood on the fringes, achingly aware that, though my every physical need was met, there was no place which I could label mine in the taken-for-granted way my half siblings and cousins did theirs. Adoption would have been an enviable, tidy experience in comparison. To see one's natural parent often, to beg with every fiber of one's being for recognition, to scream silently for a single word—it was a nightmare unrelenting.

As a teenager, I laid aside the Pollyanna role. The small boarding school I attended rocked with my carefree abandon, which spewed forth in senseless misdemeanors, destroying the even tenor of my grandparents' disciplined lives. I had no mercy, though once, arriving home in disgrace, I caught a glimpse of what I was doing to them. The small school had decided, with good reason, that I was more trouble than I was worth and bundled me off on the train for home. Arriving in the St. Johnsbury station in the wee hours of the morning, I walked into the nearly deserted room and saw my grandparents sitting quietly in the stillness waiting for me. Their backs were toward me, and they did not know of my arrival. For a moment I stood there, struck briefly with my own senseless cruelty, but the ne'er-do-well spirit I'd acquired asserted itself, and I moved toward them braced cockily for any reproof on their part. None was forthcoming. They had a dignity about them that gave me room to make an utter fool of myself and still be loved. My grandparents believed that if you treated a person as a sane adult, eventually she would become one. (While I am not sure it always works, I raised my own children in the same way. I could not do otherwise.)

Always on those rare occasions when I saw my father, I *hoped*. Hoped he'd see my mother in me and remember his youthful love. Hoped my devil-may-care attitude would at least spark his interest, or even his disdain. Hoped he would tell me something about my mother—what their dreams had been.

Once it almost happened. When Gram died in November of my sixteenth year, I was sitting alone in the darkness of my grandfather's office struggling with the nameless terror of my loss, and he came and sat beside me. Hesitantly, the words coming hard and slow, he said he'd wronged me and he knew it. It was not fair he stated, that I'd lost both mother and grandmother.

And, I, who had waited so long, could not converse with this stranger. "It's all right," I replied, "I understand," when it wasn't all right and I didn't understand at all.

He was relieved, and promised he'd write to me away at school (by then they had relented and taken me back). Perhaps if I had turned into his arms and cried, the wall between us might have crumbled, but I could not. I feared his rejection, knowing I could not survive it. Better to take what I had and be content (and, oh, how that fear has colored all the relationships of my life).

For months I reached into my post office box with trust, until at last I accepted that his promise had been but a whim of the moment, his better nature momentarily fanned into life by our shared sorrow.

After that, I stopped hoping. The next summer when my grandfather prepared to visit his son on a fine Sunday morning, I said quietly, "I am not going with you." He looked at me uncomprehendingly. For seventeen years I had visited in my father's home, feeling ugly of face and form and alien in spirit. My half brothers and sisters I had watched grow up, feeling certain the younger ones did not even know we shared a drop of common blood. Never would I expose myself to that torture again. Gramp's eyes filled with tears. Since my grandmother's death he did not like to be separated from me during the brief periods I was home from school. My resolution wavered. I knew he did not understand. He loved his son and he loved me. The solution which he and my grandmother had provided for my awkward presence in the world after my mother's death seemed a sensible one to his practical New England mind.

"I cannot do it any longer, Gramp. It has been hard for me all these years."

My grandfather accepted my simple explanation, and as we rode to the friend's house where I would spend the day, a new feeling rose between us. Not a troubled one, just a new one. In that one firm decision, I stepped out of childhood. Old age, with all its accompanying misery and heartache, was nibbling at my grandfather's heels. I longed to take him in my arms and thank him for his reserved fathering through the years, but our family did not operate that way. We learned to read a lot in silences and glances, however, and when I left the car and wished him a pleasant day, I think he heard my unspoken words. After that he didn't go to visit his son often when I was home. Maybe he understood more than I dared hope.

All this I poured into the patient ears of my young husband through torrents of tears, unleashed by the freedom, at last, to verbalize it all. The anger, the terrible pain, the hopelessness, which had consumed my youth. He listened and held me until, finally, I calmed to occasional sobs. Then he said, so very gently, "That's all behind you now. *I* am your family."

And I accepted the gift of his total, protective, tender love. Somehow I let go of all those people who were mine by blood (except my grandfather, who remained my staunch and loyal friend until his death at 89). It was restful not to care anymore. Not to pretend I was one of them, when I wasn't. Not to give love without feeling love in return.

Don's gift included more than himself. His mother became my mother, his aunts and uncles mine. They saw me as a young woman of promise and were proud of my scanty achievements. I blossomed in their midst. No longer did I need to squander time and energy attempting to be either saint or rebel. At last I could relax and sort out who I really was. It was pleasant, and for days at a time I'd forget the green hills of Vermont and all they represented. No, that's not true. I never forgot the green hills. Often at night I'd lie beside my sleeping husband and think of the valley in which I'd lived. How it looked in winter, the towering spruces black against white snow. And in summer with the stubble of the shorn fields and dusty black-eyed Susans along the dirt road.

Surrounded by western New York's flat, fertile farm lands, I missed the streams and rock-strewn hillsides of my childhood. But I *did* sometimes forget, briefly, the ones who had peopled the first act of my life. Then, walking home after my day's work in an office, I'd see myself reflected in a store window and know I was a Kimball. No amount of love and a marriage license could change that. New England to the core, my genes dictated a reserved conservatism totally foreign to the more gracious, easygoing New Yorkers with whom I rubbed shoulders day by day. I mourned them then, those kin who were rightfully mine and forever lost to me. Years later, I wrote a book about them, honestly and ruthlessly, yet found when the book was done the ink of compassion had flowed, amongst the anger, from my pen, because I loved them still.

Now, flying homeward, I understood more clearly why I had felt the compulsion to tramp along the shores of Maine. I was searching, still searching, for that elusive assurance that I was welcome on this planet, that I really belonged. It pained me to think my own adopted children might limp through life with our love never quite patching the hole of that original rejection (which usually is not rejection at all, but always feels like it).

Up here, so high above the earth, somehow it didn't much matter which corner of the great sprawling expanse of land and water had been one's birthplace. Perhaps it didn't even matter which human beings had brought one into existence. We were all so insignificant, scurrying about upon that rebel ball hung precariously in space. The miracle was that we lived at all. This God's-eye view of our weary old planet began to put a lot of things in their proper perspective. If I traced my lineage back far enough, I was a child of God, not only by creation but by special purchase. Nailed to the tree He had created, by the men He came to save, He purchased me back from my sinner's heritage. And He'd purchased my father, too. He loved us both, just as my grandfather had. It occurred to me that the bitterness I'd nursed for a lifetime toward my parent might well have saddened the heart of One who found him well worth dying for. I needed so much of His compassion, His understanding, His forgiveness, myself. How could I deny that same empathy to another? Why couldn't I just say I had loved my dad a lot and let it go at that? Jesus had come unto His own, and His own had received Him not, but He didn't rail about it the rest of His life. He just said, "I love you" to us all, without weighing and measuring the affection received in return. Maybe that's the hardest thing, to say "I care about you. You are important to me," to someone who *should* respond but doesn't. One must dispense with pride and expose oneself to pain, but perhaps that's what real love is all about. Jesus, looking down from the cross with His immortal words "Father, forgive them; for they know not what they do," practiced such love. Could we do less than our Lord?

So as the plane eased down over Boston harbor, its landing gear dropping noisily into position, I said to my long-dead father,

"I loved you, Max Kimball. The reasons why you didn't love me in return don't matter. I understand, at last, that's not what real love is all about.

"I thank you for giving me life. For choosing a girl as my mother who was filled with creativity and who willed that priceless gift to me. *You* gave me gifts, too. An easy smile, a sense of humor, a genuine liking for people that has resulted in delightful friendships. I ask your forgiveness for hating you sometimes, though the truth is I experienced a lot more sadness than anger.

"Though you grew old and ill and pathetic, I remember you as young and laughing. Always you came into a room and filled it with your presence. I was proud you were my father. I never had to see you destroyed with alcohol as your other children did. To me you were perfect and golden and right.

"This day I reach out and touch you, so very shyly. I never touched you in my life. If you move away, it no longer matters, because I know now a better kind of love."

The plane braked to a stop, and I entered the hurly-burly of Boston airport, having no idea whether I'd find a flight to Rochester or not. But it didn't really matter. Some strings, long hopelessly knotted in my life, had fallen, almost in spite of me, into kinky, but well separated, strands. I walked through the airport straight and tall, Max Kimball's daughter whether he liked it or not. I thought he would have chuckled at the idea.

Yes, Allegheny did have an empty seat on a flight to Rochester, leaving in forty-five minutes. Finding a phone, I dialed Don's office and announced my time of arrival.

"I'll be there," he said, his voice level, loving, pleased.

We'd come a long way together, this man and I. I wondered how our marriage rated on a scale of one to ten. Since I'd never been married to anyone else, I didn't have much to compare it with. We'd both come from poor families, from people who'd pinched pennies and survived the depression with such grace and good humor that neither of us ever knew we'd passed through poverty. Don was thrifty. I, weary of the parched years, longed to be a free spender. Somehow, in his low key way, he bent the 19-year-old twig into submission and we prospered. In time I learned to budget and do the banking and took pride in our healthy little savings account. Early on, we decided not to practice economy in our dealings with God. We'd never been religious teenagers, though we'd attended church and gone through all the motions. Not long after our marriage, however, we read together (and, I say reverently, only heaven knows why) Ellen White's Conflict of the Ages Series. We came out of that encounter changed. I don't know how Don would describe *his* experience, but I was "born again," however charismatic that may sound. I made a simple, trusting commitment to Jesus Christ, and though I've had moments of sin and separation since, the original bonding stands fast. Out of our new experience came a genuine desire to support the Lord's work generously and consistently. Firmly we believed He'd stand behind His promise in Malachi 3:10 and meet our needs. And He always has, not just barely, but pressed down and running over. No, Don and I never quarreled over money.

But we hadn't agreed about everything. Areas of conflict had arisen. But slowly, reluctantly, we'd learned to accept what we could not change. Sometimes we found a place of compromise. A lifestyle emerged—not perfect, but our own.

His Victorian child-raising methods appalled me, and he looked disdainfully on my determination to guide the children with love and reason. Behind our bedroom door, again and again, we wrestled quietly with this disparity in our parenting, both wise enough to know that we could not fight the war before the children. The friction ripped and tore at our marriage, but the union held. I'm sure we didn't fool the children. Many times they must have known that one or the other of us walked away from a disciplinary confrontation frustrated and unhappy. But I hope they also realized we did not let it destroy us or the relationship we'd built. Children usually understand and accept more about us than we dare hope. Perhaps it's good for them to discover that two people who have made a love commitment can disagree without the love disintegrating.

Often Don and I would discuss, heatedly, at the table, a news item, a personal philosophy, or how to deal with one problem or another. The children would listen and watch, interested, cautious. Eventually, Don, noting their silence, would laugh and say, "Your mother and I aren't fighting. Eat. We're just debating. It's good to have opinions and defend them, even loudly, if you want to. It doesn't mean we are angry."

The children would grin and go back to their food, but they didn't stop listening. My pacifist approach to life and Don's more militant one were their options. Interestingly, today, they are less peace-loving than I, less aggressive than he, as though they'd found a comfortable path between our two extremes.

Though we struggled through the brier patches of our differing temperaments, we found places of sunlight too. Just as we had freedom to defend our convictions, so there was freedom in other areas also. Freedom for both of us to pursue our own interests, spend money if the need or desire arose, to go and come as we pleased (though neither of us often chose to go). This very journey from which I was returning was a gift of freedom. A marriage can survive only when both partners have room to grow without fear or pressure from the other. God operates the universe on the same principle, and we need to adopt His policy when setting up our homes.

When a marriage holds over many years, it becomes the framework for other areas of one's life. All other interests and pursuits have value only in the context of the partner's response. The painting classes I so enjoy are enhanced by Don's surprise when I actually create something pleasing to the eye. And he needs me there to rejoice or commiserate when his golf game has been better or worse than usual. Thus my fears. How does one function when the other is gone? That's a risk I'll have to live with. If I am left behind, I'll learn then about my long-range powers of survival (I'd not done very well those many years ago when Don went off to war). In the meantime, how sad to muddy all the good times with my dread of the unknown. Somehow I'd try to leave that fear here in the Boston airport like a crumpled gum wrapper.

I'd go home and walk our fifty-two acres with him—like Adam and Eve we'd praise God for sunlight on the pond and wildflowers in the woods. We'd stroll beneath the tall spruces we'd planted with our own hands, and maybe next spring we'd begin to landscape the ravine. That had been our dream when we scouted the territory before buying the place. Looking down into the tangled jungle that divided the hillside behind the barns, we'd said, "If all those wild grapevines were removed and a few more evergreens were planted, that would be a lovely place." But we'd raised children instead, and built additions on the house and cultivated too-large vegetable gardens, and the ravine was still a jungle. Someone, years before, had tossed a few myrtle plants in the upper end, and the hardy greenery had taken root and wandered over a large expanse. So we had a beginning. I'd long seen the miniature valley in my mind's eye as it could be, bright with daffodils and flowering shrubs, fragile evergreens feathering the hillsides among the bass and black walnuts. A good project indeed for the years ahead.

Soon we'd be able to travel, and perhaps I'd ditch my thrift and find a cleaning person once again. If I were going to be of value to my family and get any writing done, I needed time and physical strength. I must fight against becoming the household drudge once more. The children had all pulled their fair share with the housework when younger. Why had I settled for less now?

Because they had jobs.

Because they were adults.

Because a neat house wasn't high on their list of priorities.

OK, I would compromise. Let their bedrooms be their private domain, as one son had long insisted they should be. If they chose to live with unmade beds and dirty socks, so be it. Neither I nor any cleaning person would invade their right to chaos. There would be two rules:

1. Their bedroom doors remained closed.

2. The rest of the house *would be* tidy. They would cooperate, and if not, they could find their own pad, though it might be difficult at the $15 weekly rate they were paying us for board and room.

With those two simple decisions, a great weight rolled from my shoulders. The war over the bedrooms had drained a great deal of my energy. Either I had cleaned them—filled with muted rage at the irony of serving children who had been well-trained to serve themselves—or I'd ignored the rooms and seethed at knowing there were corners of my house which I'd not care to have anyone see. I still didn't like the options, but I determined to live with my solution, reminding myself it was only temporary. Grown children do not live beneath the family roof forever. When they left I'd have to struggle with loneliness, which would be worse, so I'd count my blessings.

*   *   *   *   *

Another plane boarding. A seat to myself. The slow rumbling over concrete. Acceleration. The airy, fairy moment of lift when one is no longer of earth, but a citizen of the sophisticated age of flight. We are seasoned travelers all. Bring on the almonds and ginger ale. None of us even crane our necks to see the tiny cars skittering over the landscape below. Only the children gape and murmur at the wonder of it all.

I think of words I wrote after my first flight years before. They still express my sentiments accurately:

"Some people fly
until the sky
is just another freeway.

But I have seen
earth's squares of green
just once,

and looking down
on field and town
saw only peace.

I wished I did not know
that there below
men kill among the flowers.

Now I was nearing home. I had done a good thing. It had been scary and exciting. Lonely and exquisitely beautiful. For six days I had searched and sorted and tried, by backing off, to see the design in my life's tapestry. When I left home it had seemed that the stitches were all helter-skelter like a child's first needlework. But I knew now that was wrong. By squinting, I had found that a pattern *was* taking shape. It bore little resemblance to the troubled, sensitive child, or to the complex girl who had emerged. Instead it was a *new* person, this woman of the tapestry, born of all she had experienced, endured, given, taken, shared, and learned. She was not less; she was more. I must learn to like her, to trust her. To be patient with her. And to spend her for the good of others.

But I could do that only if I forgave her, freed her, listened to her. I must be at peace with her. Instinctively, I knew only God could bring that acceptance about.

For years, I'd scrutinized all family relationships. Wept for my father's unattainable love, mourned the loss of my grandmother's nurturing, struggled to mold my poor husband into an unrealistic perfection, loved my children too fiercely and too protectively. I tried to drain from everyone some vital elixir that would slake the thirst of my loneliness and discontent. Here in the sky, serenely caught between heaven and earth, I knew it was everyone's thirst. Cut off from God, we are a million raw nerve ends screaming into the blackness. The cross glows with hope in the night sky, and we cling to its luster, soothed and comforted by its message, but not quite made whole. We will never be totally whole till we feel His touch, see approval and acceptance in His eyes. Till we know whatever it is He wants of us has been met. *I say that reverently.*

God is a mystery in spite of all the Bible's attempts to define Him. Sometimes He's the gentleness of Jesus holding a child, and sometimes He's Yahweh piercing into our sin-riddled souls with an intensity that leaves us quaking at His feet.

We have a thousand questions, and from the pulpits

thunder a barrage of answers, jarring in their lack of unity. But Yahweh is still. We must find our own answers, not sifting and sorting among the confusions of men, but alone upon our knees, or with our Bibles open before us. For there I've found Yahweh whispers answers now and then. Soft as angels' wings they hint of something so healing, so pure, so future, that one clings to the memory when the storms of religious controversy lower.

I fear those who have the reality of the gospel all neatly tied and packaged. Either they are extremely far ahead of me or they are only fooling themselves. If their assurance truly signifies an advanced spiritual state, then I beg their patience and compassion. But if, on the other hand, they possess a false confidence, then let me exercise patience and compassion, for their situation is yet more pitiful than mine.

Now I must go home and expose myself to the only avenues of communication we have with divinity. I must not let my own failures as a Christian distract me or the ease of less demanding routines entice me away. It would be fatal to fall back into the old despairs.

Will I retain the insights of this week, carrying them into the household hassle, my marriage, my parenting, my Christian fellowship? I must simply remember that God is making something of me as fast as I will let Him. That I can hasten the process by accepting His methods and listening for His leading. And by being in those places where He speaks most readily, however faintly. My ear must ever be tuned for that "still small voice."

* * * * *

The plane lowers over familiar territory. Rochester, the city of lilacs and Eastman School of Music. A cultural town. But Rochester is not home. Across the fall countryside, fine highways beckon the traveler toward Buffalo, Rochester's rowdier industrial sister.

A LITTLE JOURNEY

And in between the two slumbers the little city of Batavia. Home. Maybe a week before I'd have said New England was home. But now, with the afternoon sun warming the rolling, scruffy countryside, I knew this small nondescript part of America was knit even more firmly into my being than the Vermont valleys of my birth. Home was that little city where I knew each street and alley. The fine and the dingy. The new library where I go to pick the brains of men, the homes of friends where I laugh and converse and sometimes shed a tear.

I wanted to drive west on Main Street at sundown and see the old brick buildings and the brand-new mall all bathed in the gold dust of evening. At church my friends would say, "You're back early. You missed us," and they'd laugh and tease me a bit.

Best of all, I'd go down Prole Road till I came to the big red barn and the pond where migrating ducks etch silver V's on the black water. The old white farmhouse would hum with youthful vitality and the warmth of welcome. They would be glad I had come home, our sons and daughters. Mostly because I was so useful, but partly, too, because my presence was security and assurance and comfort, however taken for granted. I was lucky. So very lucky. We are all lucky if someone is glad when we come home.

When I walked into the airport terminal, I saw him before he did me. I no longer knew whether he was handsome or plain. He was simply mine. I wore my new red shirt with its pewter sea gull pin and was his woman, battered and scarred with living, but stronger and wiser than his bride had been. We would venture together into the future. Into eternity, God willing.

Then I said his name, and he turned, smiling, moving quickly toward me. When his arms enfolded me, I had, indeed, come home.